The Centre for Co-operation with European Economies in Transition, which was created in March 1990, is the focal point for co-operation between the OECD and Central and Eastern European countries. Its major responsibility is to design and manage a programme of policy advice and technical assistance which puts the expertise of the Secretariat and Member countries at the disposal of countries engaged in economic reform. this advice or assistance can take numerous forms, including conferences, seminars, missions and workshops in order to explore policy questions or review draft legislation; it can also include training for government officials who are called to implement market-oriented policies.

In December 1990 the Council adopted a programme "Partners in Transition" for the purpose of providing more focused assistance to those countries (the Czech and Slovak Federal Republic, Hungary and Poland) that are more advanced in introducing market-oriented reforms and desire to become members of OECD. Additional activities which the Centre would co-ordinate under this programme could include reviews of the country's general economic situation and prospects, reviews of issues and policies in specific areas and participation in certain OECD Committees.

In all these activities, the Centre maintains close relations with other multilateral bodies such as the G-24 co-ordinated by the Commission of the European Communities, the International Monetary Fund, the World Bank, the European Bank for Reconstruction and Development and the Economic Commission for Europe, with the mutual objective of ensuring the complementarity of respective efforts to support economic reforms in Central and Eastern Europe.

The OECD's Working Group on Accounting Standards contributed to the organisation of the Seminar, in the framework of the Centre's work programme, as part of its work on encouraging the harmonisation of accounting standards.

The report is published under the responsibility of the Secretary-General of OECD.

ALSO AVAILABLE

Statistics for a Market Economy (1991)
(14 91 04 1) ISBN 92-64-13486-7   FF150   £20   US$36   DM58
Transformation of Planned Economies: Property Rights Reform and Macroeconomic Stability (1991)
(14 91 03 1) ISBN 92-64-13491-3   FF125   £16   US$30   DM48
Economic Survey of Hungary (1991)
(09 92 01 1) ISBN 92-64-13554-5   FF90   £32   US$52   DM95
The Role of Tax Reform in Central and Eastern European economies (1991)
(14 91 05 1) ISBN 92-64-13575-8   FF280   £40   US$68 DM115

"Accounting Standards Harmonization Series No. 5"
    Consolidated Financial Statements (1988) Bilingual
    (21 88 05 3) ISBN 92-64-03141-3   FF50   £6   US$11   DM22
"Accounting Standards Harmonization Series No. 6"
    New Financial Instruments (1991) Bilingual
    (21 91 02 3) ISBN 92-64-03508-7   FF70   £9   US$16   DM27

Cut along dotted line

ORDER FORM

Please enter my order for:

Qty.	Title	OECD Code	Price
....	....	....	....
....	....	....	....
....	....	....	....
....	....	....	....
		Total :	....

- Payment is enclosed ☐
- Charge my VISA card ☐   Number of card ....
  (Note: You will be charged the French franc price.)
  Expiration of card .... Signature ....
- *Send invoice. A purchase order is attached* ☐

Send publications to *(please print):*
    Name ....
    Address ....
    ....
    ....

    Send this Order Form to OECD Publications Service, 2, rue André-Pascal, 75775 PARIS CEDEX 16, France, or to OECD Publications and Information Centre or Distributor in your country *(see last page of the book for addresses).*

Prices charged at the OECD Bookshop.

THE OECD CATALOGUE OF PUBLICATIONS and supplements will be sent free of charge on request addressed either to OECD Publications Service, or to the OECD Distributor in your country.

Contents

6

Preface

In September 1990 the Centre for Co-operation with European Economies in Transition, with the co-operation of members of the Working Group on Accounting Standards and the Fédération des experts-comptables européens, held a seminar on Accounting Reforms in Central and Eastern Europe. Experts from the Czech and Slovak Federal Republic, Hungary, Poland and the USSR took part in these discussions together with participants from the accounting profession, academics, the business and labour community and international organisations. In identifying the objectives and the main elements of financial reporting, as well as the accounting issues relating to restructuring, privatisation and the development of financial markets, the seminar fell squarely in the context of the overall economic reforms taking place in central and eastern European countries and the role of the OECD Centre in assisting those reforms.

In market economies, accounting provides the economic information necessary for efficient decision-making by everyone — workers, consumers, shareholders, potential investors, home and host governments, and the general public. Centrally planned economies use accounting only to satisfy national planning and public policy requirements. The introduction of market oriented reforms creates new groups of users, and pressure builds to reform accountancy practices in order to meet the information needs of these users. This seminar identified who are the new parties which now need information on the performance and financial positions of enterprises, as well as what information they require — for what purposes and in what forms.

The reform process varies among different countries, with authorisation of east-west joint ventures prevalent in some (the USSR, for example), and the privatisation and restructuring of state-owned enterprises already well underway in others, (such as Poland and Hungary). Whatever the type and degree of change, legal and economic reforms generally cannot ignore the necessity of also reforming accounting systems — prerequisite for the introduction of capital markets, and a catalyst for the efficient functioning of the corporate sector and the promotion of foreign direct investment. The participants at this seminar had the opportunity to exchange information on the reforms under way and how they affect the accounting practices.

The OECD is particularly well placed to provide this kind of dialogue and international co-operation. The Working Group on Accounting Standards, which was set up by the Committee on International Investment and Multinational Enterprises, has worked actively since 1979 to develop clarifications of the accounting terms contained in the chapter on disclosure of information of the Guidelines for Multinational Enterprises and to promote efforts towards international comparability of financial statements and harmonisation of accounting standards.

This seminar addressed topics of major concern for policy-makers involved in the reform and restructuring of centrally planned economies. On the basis of the issues identified, the OECD is developing proposals for future co-operation.

Robert Cornell
Deputy Secretary-General

Introduction

Accounting Reforms in Central and Eastern Europe: Main Issues

OECD Secretariat

Introduction

In an accelerating process of reform, several countries in Eastern Europe are moving from a centrally planned economy towards a market economy system. A first step in this transition has been made by authorisation of east-west joint ventures. In several countries, programmes for privatisation and restructuring of state-owned enterprises have been launched.

Accounting is a form of communication, and accounting standards reflect the general economic and legal infrastructure of business transactions. As this environment is changing, accounting systems rooted in concepts of centrally planned economies are no longer viable. Accounting reform is a major element in legal and economic reform and a prerequisite for the introduction of capital markets, the promotion of investment, and the efficient functioning of the corporate sector.

Fundamental concepts of financial reporting

The purpose of accounting is to provide information on business activities in order to facilitate decision-making by users of financial statements. To the extent that accounting systems are designed to meet the needs of users, objectives and fundamental concepts of accounting and financial reporting are influenced by the structure of the economic system.

A. Financial reporting in market economies

In market economies, the basic objective of financial reporting of business enterprises is to provide information on the performance, the financial position, and changes in the financial position of an enterprise. This information refers to the needs of a variety of users, such as present and potential investors, creditors, suppliers, employees, government. Financial accounting also provides input into management accounting systems.

11

The wide range of interests involved explains differences of emphasis in the accounting systems of Member countries. In some countries (USA, United Kingdom, Canada and Australia for example) the need of investors in the capital markets has played the most important role in the development of accounting standards. Accordingly, the predominant objective of financial statements in these countries is to provide information on the performance of the enterprise, which enables investors to decide whether to buy, hold or sell a share in the company. In other countries, the predominant purpose of accounting is to calculate the profit (or loss) which is distributable to shareholders while simultaneously providing protection of creditors. This applies to accounting in countries like Germany, Switzerland and Japan, where the protection of creditors plays an important role.

To be technically perfect, standard-setting and harmonisation would have to be unaffected by external influences. But governments have to take into account the needs of national accounting statistics, as well as social and taxation questions. The influence of these factors on the establishment of accounting standards varies according to the degree of government intervention.

One significant example of the way in which external influences impinge is that of taxation. The relationship between taxation and financial reporting is determined according to three main options: uniformity, separation and adjustment. Uniformity is undesirable, since the objectives of taxation and reporting are not the same. Taxation looks at the past to assess an enterprise's performance in order to determine its taxable income. Financial reporting is an aid to future decision-making and calls for flexibility incompatible with requirements of tax legislation. And when tax rules are specially designed to meet the objectives of national economic policy, the rules governing reporting for tax purposes may derogate from the rules and principles of financial reporting.

Accounting, therefore, is an instrument designed to serve a variety of purposes carrying different weights among OECD countries, but complying with the same general objective: to provide a true and fair view of the performance, the financial position and changes in the financial position of an enterprise.

Among the basic accounting principles applied by business enterprises in OECD countries are:

— the accrual concept
— the going-concern concept
— the consistency principle
— the substance over form principle.

In addition, the concept of prudence exerts a significant influence on measurement and accounting methods used for the preparation of financial statements.

According to the accrual concept, the effects of business transactions are recognised when they occur (and independently from cash received or paid). Transactions are recorded in the books and shown in the financial statements of the period to which they relate.

The going-concern concept assumes that the reporting enterprise will continue in operation for the foreseeable future.

The substance-over-from principle requires that business transactions and other events be accounted for and presented in accordance with their substance and financial reality and not merely with their legal form.

The consistency-principle requires that accounting policies be continued from one balance sheet date to the next in a consistent manner. Any changes should be restricted to exceptional cases and should be explained adequately.

Business transactions are surrounded by uncertainty. This should be recognised by exercising prudence when preparing financial statements. On the other hand, application of prudence cannot justify the creation of hidden reserves.

B. Accounting and reporting in centrally planned economies

In centrally planned economies the objective of accounting and reporting is to provide information which is necessary for central planning and control of the national economy.

Financial accounting is an element in the information system designed to help government agencies in planning, allocating resources and monitoring plan fulfilment. Thus, reporting of business enterprises is primarily addressed to government authorities. To a large extent, reporting provides statistical data to enable government authorities to control productivity in quantitative terms.

For this reason, the basic accounting principles in a centrally planned economy are different from those usually applied within the OECD. For example, the accrual concept is not adhered to. Business transactions are accounted for on a cash basis, recognising revenues and expenses when received or paid. Therefore, calculation of profit is not comparable to OECD accounting systems.

In central and eastern european countries accounting and reporting is meant to supply data which can be summarised to provide a condensed view of the aggregate activities of enterprises by region, industry and the entire economy. In order to achieve this, accounting policies and procedures of book-keeping are laid down in detailed regulations for every significant business transaction.

The standardised accounting and reporting system includes:

—   a uniform chart of accounts (designed under a macro-economic approach instead of an enterprise level approach);

—   authorised procedures for the recording and classification of data in the accounting records;

—   standardised forms for the internal documentation and the reports to government authorities.

C. Accounting issues arising in the context of the transition to market economies

As the economic system in Central and Eastern Europe is changing towards a market system, accounting standards have to be changed accordingly. To the extent that new groups of users (e.g. investors and creditors) require information on the financial position and performance of an enterprise, accounting regulations in central and eastern european countries should reflect their needs as well as the needs of government.

This leads to the necessity of preparing financial statements in accordance with generally accepted accounting principles applied in market economies. Difficult problems will have to be solved, for example, the revaluation of assets leading to the elimination of the influence of previous state controlled prices as well as of overvaluation of plant, machinery and equipment which had been stipulated by governmental instructions. In the context of the privatisation of state-owned enterprises, a clear distinction between equity and debt will have to be introduced into the balance sheet.

When elaborating new accounting and reporting regulations, central and eastern european countries can benefit from the experience of standard setting bodies in OECD Member countries and international organisations. In this context, the accounting profession, through its representative bodies, can make a major contribution.

Main elements of financial reporting

A. The legal infrastructure of accounting and reporting

Accounting is strongly influenced by its legal environment.

Important issues are:
— the development of capital markets
— the permission to carry out corporate activities
— regulations concerning corporate finance
— the repatriation of profits and capital invested
— property rights.

B. Balance sheet layout and valuation principles

The balance sheet layout in most of the centrally planned economies compares groups of assets with sources of financing (funds) and liabilities in order to indicate whether financial rules are followed by the respective enterprise. For example, the net book value of fixed assets is to be financed by the "statutory fund". Investment in fixed assets has to be financed by investment funds and bank loans. The investment fund (sometimes called funds for promotion of production, science and technology) is made up of retained earnings. The balance sheet also contains a large number of items entered according to the "gross entry" principle, such as fixed assets on the assets side and the accumulated depreciation fund on the funds and liabilities side. Social funds may be formed to provide material incentives for staff (comparable to a thirteenth salary or bonus) and to increase social welfare. The assets related to these funds (usually specific bank accounts) are to be used exclusively for the purposes for which those funds have been set up.

In OECD Member countries, the balance sheet of private enterprises is usually not subject to rules of funding. Total assets are financed by owners' equity and liabilities without any link to individual balance sheet items. A distinction between owners' equity and liabilities does exist. In the case of uncertain liabilities or contingencies, adequate provisions are made and shown on the liabilities side.

With respect to valuation, the historical cost principle is common practice in OECD as well as in central and eastern european countries, although exceptions exist. In several Central and Eastern European countries, periodical and occasional changes in prices of finished goods (as stipulated by government) are also reflected in accounting records. Adjustments to the book values of fixed assets are carried out from time to time. The book values of imported raw materials and machinery may be influenced by the government "price stabilisation" measures and its foreign trade monopoly. Depreciation rules and periods are much longer than in OECD economies. The recorded value of fixed assets is often overvalued.

Finished goods and work in progress are usually accounted for at historical cost. In OECD Member countries effective production cost is normally used for the valuation of inventories, but various interpretations of "production cost" exist with respect to the inclusion of production and the other overheads. Selling expenses and research and development costs are not usually included. Inventories are written down to their net realisable value if historical cost exceeds the estimated selling price less the costs of completion and estimated selling expenses.

In central and eastern european countries, inventories are accounted for at total cost, including general overheads and selling costs. The production cost is often calculated on the basis of standard costing and budgeting. If total cost of finished goods exceeds the net realisable value, the respective items are to be accounted for at budgeted cost. Work in progress is carried at cost. Provisions for expected losses, are unusual.

C. Income statement and profit allocation

The general purposes of income statements are:

— to determine the financial result for a period by comparison of revenues and other income against the related expenditure;
  and

— to complement the balance sheet by providing details of the components and sources of the result for the accounting period.

In OECD countries there are two models for the calculation of profit or loss:

— the total cost model
  and

— the cost of sales model.

Both models yield the same result.

15

The total cost method presents primary costs as they occurred during the period, irrespective of whether or not the goods produced were actually sold in the market. The corresponding layout of the income statement gives a breakdown of all costs incurred by type of expenditure (materials, wages and salaries, depreciation). In order to calculate a result from realised sales, appropriate adjustment of cost is achieved by crediting an increase of inventories at production cost to the profit and loss account as a separate item. The cost of sales method compares revenues from sales with costs of goods sold. Costs are grouped by operational functions (production, distribution and general administration).

In centrally planned economies (the Soviet Union, for example), a different model is used for the income statement which is — to a certain extent — comparable to the cost of sales method. Major differences exist as regards items treated as cost which would be treated as profit allocation (allocation to certain funds, for example) in income statements in OECD countries.

D. Specific accounting rules applying to joint ventures

As a rule, joint ventures apply accounting principles which comply with the national standards of the host country. On the other hand, the venturer needs financial statements in accordance with the accounting standards used in his home country. For consolidation purposes, financial statements of a joint venture are subject to certain corrections to unify the layout of the balance sheet and the profit and loss account.

In the context of east-west joint ventures reforms have taken place in some central and eastern european countries in order to incorporate the needs of western joint venture partners. An important question is how far these reforms meet the requirements of both, the domestic and the foreign partner.

In some central and eastern european countries, accounting and reporting policies applied by joint ventures may deviate from national practice in order to reflect the needs of the foreign partner. For example, assets contributed as capital by the joint venture partners may be recorded at the value agreed in the memorandum of association. With the permission of the government, depreciation periods may be fixed in accordance with the policies applied by the western partner.

Calculation and distribution of profit are major issues in the context of accounting of east-west joint ventures. This refers to the policies concerning recognition of revenues and expenses, depreciation rules, provisions the creation of funds. According to the national law in some Eastern European countries, east-west joint ventures are required to create special purpose funds in the same manner as domestic (state-owned) enterprises. The use of these funds is limited to their respective purposes; their distribution to shareholders is prohibited. Allocations to these funds can usually be deducted from taxable income. In addition, most countries in Central and Eastern Europe offer fiscal incentives in order to attract foreign investors.

Foreign currency transactions in central and eastern european countries are restricted, because their currencies are not convertible. Therefore, the repatriation of the western partner's share of profit is normally only possible by using the joint venture's own foreign currency accounts unless the free transfer of profits is guaranteed by an agreement with the government of the host country.

Other possibilities for the repatriation of profit are to buy and export goods manufactured in the host country or to buy foreign currency at official foreign currency auctions.

Accounting issues relating to restructuring, privatisation and the development of financial markets

A. *Accounting as a management tool*

The information needs of management when making operational decisions refer primarily to costs. This information has to be:

— promptly available
— summarised or detailed as appropriate
— shaped in a manner suitable for the respective problems.

Therefore, cost accounting (sometimes called "management accounting") applies principles different from those applied by financial accounting. In the western countries cost accounting principles are formulated individually by management. However, financial and cost accounting are linked together. For example, financial accounting supplies input data to cost accounting and cost accounting supplies data needed as a basis for the evaluation of inventories.

In Central and Eastern Europe as well as in OECD Member countries, financial and cost accounting systems are integrated systems. It is questionable, however, whether cost accounting principles applied by enterprises in a centrally planned economy would be sufficient for management tasks in privatised enterprises and in joint ventures. In centrally planned economies, usually no distinction has been made between marginal and fixed costs. As a result, no answer can be provided to the question as to how far costs will increase or decrease when production quantity is changed, or what contribution to cover fixed costs is made by different products.

In OECD Member countries, management accounting is an integral component of the "controlling function" in an enterprise. In modern business management controlling is a sub-system of management which co-ordinates planning, controls, and the supply of information systematically and in this way supports the management of the enterprise.

In western enterprises, management accounting is subject to cost-effectiveness-analyses. Therefore, information procedures carried out by management accounting departments are focused on items that are considered essential by the management of the enterprise; usually no regulations are stipulated by government concerning management accounting. In centrally planned economies, however, the management function is — to a certain extent — transferred to government. Thus, cost accounting is determined by governmental regulations.

B. *Disclosure rules, prospectuses and availability of financial statements*

Financial statements of enterprises in OECD Member countries are subject to disclosure requirements stipulated by corporate law and accounting standards.

17

Additional and more detailed requirements apply to prospectuses which are to be published by companies applying for registration on securities exchanges.

Thus far, Hungary is the only country in Eastern Europe in which stock markets have been established, although projects are currently under consideration. While disclosure rules, registration procedures and requirements for prospectuses are subject to harmonisation and mutual recognition among OECD Member countries, such regulations are yet to be developed in Eastern European countries.

Companies of central and eastern european countries may issue stocks and other securities on western capital markets. In this case they have to meet the disclosure and registration requirements applying in these markets.

Financial statements of companies listed on securities exchanges in western countries are to be published in newspapers or official bulletins and are also available as a brochure from the company's headquarters. In several OECD Member countries financial statements of listed companies and the notes thereto are to be filed additionally with the securities exchange authority requiring a specific form of presentation.

In a number of central european countries the requirement to publish financial statements applies not only to listed companies but also to any company of a certain size. Disclosure of the company's financial statements is justified on grounds of economic significance, irrespective of how it is legally constituted.

C. Valuation rules: assets and liabilities

In the medium and long term, restructuring and privatisation of enterprises in Central and Eastern Europe will stimulate economic growth. Investments in modernising the corporate sector are to be financed by shareholders and creditors. Credit standing and stock quality are usually judged on the basis of information provided in financial statements. If these statements do not give a true and fair view of the performance and the financial situation of the enterprise, such an assessment is not possible. Thus, financial statements of enterprises to be privatised in eastern european countries should be restated for two reasons:

1) creditors from OECD countries will judge credit standing according to their knowledge of, and experience with accounting standards which are generally accepted in the OECD area;

2) shareholders are normally interested in future earnings per share and, therefore, are not willing to be exposed to risk resulting from events prior to their involvement nor to losses resulting from writing down assets to their fair value.

According to accounting principles which are generally accepted in OECD Member countries, the valuation of fixed assets should reflect their ability to generate future profits. In the transition to a market economy system, a revaluation of fixed assets, ie., machinery, will be necessary according to their productivity. The revaluation of assets and provisions by applying accounting principles used in some OECD Member countries, such as the lower of cost or market principle may even yield a negative amount of owners' equity. In the context of privatisation of enterprises a negative amount of equity may be balanced by compensation claims against state agencies.

Within eastern european countries different rules apply to the ownership of land. In several countries east-west joint ventures and private enterprises are allowed to purchase land. Generally credit standing enterprises being privatised should have the right to purchase land because western creditors usually request mortgages as security. In countries where enterprises may only obtain a temporary right to use land and other natural resources by payment of a fixed amount, the question arises as to how these rights of usage should be accounted for (lease accounting).

The accounting profession

A. The role and organisation of the profession

There are major differences in the role and organisation of the accounting profession between OECD and Central and Eastern European countries. In a market economy, accountants act as independent auditors, tax and management consultants. These services require a high degree of competence and experience. Independent auditing plays a major role in the capital markets. Since users of financial statements must be able to rely on the information disclosed by enterprises, an independent audit is necessary. The qualification of auditors is ensured by legislation and rules established by professional bodies. Auditing is exercised as a private professional activity.

In centrally planned economies, accountants are employees of industrial enterprises. The chief accountant in an enterprise is responsible not only for accounting and reporting but also for the compliance of the enterprise with regulations and the central planning objectives. Audit procedures are carried out by government authorities or may be delegated to authorised auditing organisations such as, for example, INAUDIT in the Soviet Union.

Almost all major international accounting firms have already established offices in central and eastern european countries or have formed joint ventures together with local accountants in order to apply for the recognition as authorised independent auditors.

In OECD as well as in central and eastern european countries, accountants have formed professional bodies to represent their interests both at national and international level. On the international level, the *Fédération des Experts-Comptables Européens* (FEE) and the *International Federation of Accountants* (IFAC) are involved in the elaboration and development of professional standards. In some central and eastern european countries, several activities have been initiated to reorganise the accounting profession. Advice is offered by international accountancy bodies such as IFAC and FEE.

B. Professional qualifications of accountants

In OECD countries accounting firms perform independent audit services, as well as tax and business consulting. With respect to the prerequisites of approval which are stipulated by legislation, accountants have to pass a professional examination. As a rule, admission to the examination is restricted to persons holding a university degree and possessing professional experience of a certain number of years. Within the EEC minimum standards for professional qualification of auditors have been established by the 8th Council Directive.

Accountants in central and eastern european countries have had less exposure than their western counterparts to auditing and consulting practice. In order to bridge this gap and introduce accountants from Central and Eastern Europe to accounting principles used in market economies, specific training programmes have been launched by the *World Bank*, the *United Nations Centre on Transnational Corporations* and by several government authorities and other institutions of OECD countries, including the FEE and other professional bodies.

C. Accounting training and research

Accounting training and research is carried out by universities and other academic institutions as well as the accounting profession, in particular accounting associations, professional bodies and large international accounting firms. After graduating from university a junior accountant benefits from on-the-job training and seminars held by experienced practitioners of his company. To keep knowledge on an appropriate level, accountants are recommended to participate in continuing professional education programmes. The IFAC has issued guidelines on professional education and training addressed to national professional bodies in order to achieve and maintain a high level of professional knowledge and qualification of accountants worldwide.

Whereas academic research in the field of accounting concentrates mostly on theoretical questions as well as international comparison of accounting standards, research on practical problems of accounting is carried out by research departments of professional bodies and larger accounting firms.

As far as professional education in Eastern European countries is concerned, accountants are qualified in accounting techniques and procedures applied in a centrally planned economy. To meet the accounting requirements of a privatised enterprise or an east-west joint venture, additional training will be necessary. Some efforts have already taken place to develop curricula for training students, practitioners and academics in western accounting techniques. The UN Centre on Transnational Corporations has elaborated such curricula in co-operation with large international accounting firms. These efforts should be further increased.

Standard setting and harmonisation of accounting standards

A. National, regional and international approaches

Capital markets and economic activities are becoming increasingly internationalised, and the number of enterprises operating on several national markets at once is constantly growing. The fact that more and more investors are anxious to purchase diversified securities and covering an increasing number of countries leads to interpenetration of capital markets. International investment is at the very heart of international economic co-operation, and financial information plays an essential role in the decision to invest. It is increasingly necessary for this information to be reliable, comparable and framed in terms of generally accepted accounting standards. Thus the international harmonisation of those standards is a matter of urgency.

The national private and public standard-setting bodies, the regional organisations, in particular the European Economic Community, and the international organisations play a fundamental role in the process of international harmonisation by the complementarity of their efforts.

At the international level the IASC has published 31 International Accounting Standards on various accounting issues. Whereas in the past numerous options of accounting treatment have been permitted, IASC has launched a process of improving the Standards by harmonising the range of permissible options. This project is designed to achieve more comparability of financial statements thereby reducing the costs of capital market transactions.

The OECD has issued Guidelines for multinational enterprises containing a chapter on disclosure of information. Disclosure requirements as stated in this chapter are to be seen as a minimum standard for multinational as well as domestic enterprises. According to the OECD Guidelines, enterprises "should publish within reasonable time limits, on a regular basis, but at least annually, financial statements and other pertinent information relating to the enterprise as a whole, comprising in particular:

1)   the structure of the enterprise, showing the name and location of the parent company, its main affiliates, including shareholdings between them;

2)   the geographical areas where operations are carried out and the principal activities carried on therein by the parent company and the main affiliates;

3)   the operating results and sales by geographical area and the sales in the major lines of business for the enterprise as a whole;

4)   significant new capital investment by geographical area and, as far as practicable, by major lines of business for the enterprise as a whole;

5)   a statement of the sources and uses of funds by the enterprise as a whole;

6)   the average number of employees in each geographical area;

7)   research and development expenditure for the enterprise as a whole;

8)   the policies followed in respect of intra-group pricing;

9)   the accounting policies, including those on consolidation, observed in compiling the published information".

The OECD Working Group on Accounting Standards acts as a catalyst for international harmonisation by identifying common concepts, seeking a consensus on the objectives to be attained and analysing the means to obtain those objectives. The United Nations Group on International Standards of Accounting and Reporting has extended this dialogue on a broad geographical basis.

Objectives and Fundamental Concepts
of Financial Reporting

Accounting and Financial Reporting in Market Economies
Allan Cook

The feature that distinguishes market from centrally planned economics is that resource allocations are determined by the price mechanism. Supplies of goods, of labour and other services and of finance have to be bought and sold competitively in the marketplace. It follows that the success and ultimately the survival of a business will depend on the effects of thousands of individual transactions.

The contribution of accounting to the market economy is made in two distinct ways: internal reporting for the purposes of management control and external financial reporting. This paper looks at some of the characteristics of each and examines possible relationships between the two.

Internal reporting

The need for advanced accounting techniques to control a business and report its transactions will vary according to the complexity of that business's processes and of the markets in which it is acting. What was suitable for the last century — or even the last decade may be seriously inadequate for the changed conditions of today. An obvious example lies in the control of inventory levels. When orders from customers are predictable or related to a standard type of product, the optimum levels at which to maintain inventories of raw materials and components are reasonably easy to determine. As competition forces the business into being able to provide a wider product range available on demand or at short notice, the precise monitoring and forecasting of inventory levels becomes critical to the success of the business. The need for action may not at first be recognised, since customer demand may be satisfied by increasing inventory levels. A sudden rise in interest rates, however, can make such levels impossible to sustain and present the business with the unattractive choice of losing customers by failing to meet orders or becoming insolvent.

The above example illustrates the central position of accounting in the process of controlling the increasing complexity of modern business. Accounting control by a business over its own activities is exercised as a two stage process:

first, *monitoring* what is happening at critical points in time for action to be taken; and

second, *planning* by quantifying and assessing the probable future effects of alternative strategies.

The precise form of monitoring (sometimes called internal reporting) that is appropriate to an enterprise will vary according to the nature of this business, the structure of the organisation and sometimes even the management style. A large manufacturing company may require a detailed costing system to monitor on a monthly, weekly or real-time basis the effects of changes in input prices, labour rates, overhead costs, volume of activity and other variances. A retailing company may be satisfied with simple divisions into direct and indirect costs grouped under a few relevant categories. What is essential in all cases is that the purpose for which accounting information will be used should determine the design of the system and that the limitations of the system should be clearly understood when attempts are made to derive information for different purposes.

The focus on purpose means that internal accounting reports should be sufficiently precise to identify the nature of emerging problems and so structured as to identify the manager responsible for taking action. This demands a continuing effort by those responsible for the reporting system to ensure that it is in fact being understood and used by managers and managed alike.

It is perhaps a truism to say that for information to lead to action it must be timely. A few advance estimates may be worth more than a book full of statistics that arrive too late or take too long to digest.

Another important feature of an effective internal reporting system is that it should be kept under continual review. Particularly during periods of rapid change, such as the control of a major expansion programme, or external instability, such as volatile prices, general inflation or rapidly changing exchange rates, a business must be able to introduce new accounting techniques to identify the new danger points and change the priorities of operational management. During the high inflation years of the mid-seventies, with apparently high profits but cash resources draining away, the business that survived were those that saw through the illusion of inflation and concentrated on cutting costs, reducing working capital and measuring their performance by indicators that adjusted for the effects of changing prices.

The exercise of planning involves a great deal more than accounting techniques but it is important that the role of these should be properly understood. There are two extreme positions to be avoided. On the one hand, it is wrong to be mesmerised by the figures in future projections. On the other hand, the impossibility of accurate prediction does not relieve a business from the task of detailed calculations. The role of accounting is to quantify and put into perspective the various uncertainties so that the risk can be better understood and in some cases reduced by immediate or later actions. A business plan may serve as a target for various layers of management but an equally important function is to educate management before the event by getting them to consider the sensitivity of the plan to a number of internal and external uncertainties. A plan needs to be drawn up on the basis of some agreed, broad economic assumptions as well as detailed predictions consistent with these about such matters as changes in market shares and movements in prices and costs. Some large organisations require their managers to consider the effects of alternative economic "scenarios", and on occasion crises scenarios, in order that the organisation may know how to react in a prompt but not frantic way when the unexpected occurs.

Two critical areas of the use of accounting techniques for planning purposes are the appraisal of investment proposals and the provision of cash flow forecasts. Sound procedures for presenting investment proposals for approval not only ensure that the financial implications are measured in the most appropriate way but assist top management in deciding between competing demands on the present and future resources of the business. It is, of course, rare for an investment proposal to be put forward in isolation. Normally, it will form part of a general strategy agreed or confirmed at the time that the business plan is approved. Nevertheless, the particular opportunities arising within the strategy need to be rigorously assessed before funds are committed to ensure that they meet the profitability criteria that have been set.

Cashflow forecasts, identifying as far as possible the expected minimum and maximum demands for funds, form an essential part of financial strategy, leading to two separate types of management action. On the operational side, the forecasts should in principle be integrated with other forms of internal reporting in order that attention can be given to expected sources of weakness. On the treasuring side, the forecasts assist the optimum structuring of the enterprises's short-term funds, borrowing or borrowing facilities. Bankers, in particular, will wish to monitor an enterprise's fluctuating cash needs in order to identify departures from plan in time to take remedial action or to limit their exposure.

Financial reporting

If the continued survival of an enterprise depends on its economic performance, there are many parties who can claim a right to receive information about that performance and the enterprise's financial position. First are the shareholders, who own the company and have invested in the expectation of a return on their investment. With similar needs, though possibly different rights, are potential investors, without whom there would be no market in the company's shares or prospect of success for any new issues of capital the company may wish to make in the future.

Other parties with a right to general financial information about the company include lenders, suppliers, employees and, for certain industries, state regulators. Some of these parties may have special information needs that distinguish them from the others. For example, lenders will wish to know what security, if any, has been given to other creditors; employees may be more interested in the prospects for their work location than in the general prosperity of the wider enterprise; a regulator will almost certainly require detailed information on prices and costs. Nevertheless, each of these special groups has a similar need to that of the shareholder for general purpose information on the performance and financial position of the enterprise as a whole.

In the past it has been common to claim that the needs of lenders and other creditors extend only to what is sometimes called a "minimum statement of financial position", in which all amounts are stated on the most conservative possible basis. For the most protected layer of creditors this may still be true but for many — particularly those committed for the long-term and large amounts — an understanding of the performance and financial position of the debtor company is as important as it is for the shareholders. The protection of such creditors lies not so much in today's balance sheet as in the quality of the company's business, its long-term strategies and the ability of its management. Judgements on matters such as these require similar information to that required by the shareholder.

The information needs of the regulator are particularly interesting, since they exemplify the public policy aspect of the provision of general purpose financial information. In privatising former state monopolies the UK Government has set up various industry regulators with the duty of setting pricing policies and other conditions of trading that encourage the newly privatised company or companies to increase efficiency while also in some cases making room for competitors to enter the market. This delicate balancing act naturally gives rise to public discussion. For this purpose, both the regulator and the regulated need to be able to refer to generally available financial information that provides a realistic picture of performance and financial position.

One party that may have an interest in the publicly available financial statements of an enterprise is the fiscal authority. In most countries it is regarded as sound public policy that the tax charge on companies should in general be based on commercial accounting principles rather than on some arbitrary formula. Difficulties arise, however, in two cases. The first is if special fiscal rules such as artificially high rates of depreciation are required to be followed in the published financial statements in order to obtain the tax concession. The second is if new accounting methods, developed in response to new commercial transactions or better insights into the purposes of accounting, are prevented from becoming part of financial reporting practice because they are resisted by the fiscal authority.

By contrast with the rapid innovations sometimes required in internal reporting, financial reporting methods usually develop rather slowly. It is, of course, much more difficult to develop a general solution to a new problem than a "quick fix" which may be sufficient for the purposes of a particular company. This difficulty explains why so many businesses managed to set up the necessary internal measures to cope with inflation, while violently disagreeing with the proposals for incorporating adjustments for changing prices into published financial statements. The principal reason, however, why financial reporting methods are comparatively slow to develop is that they are rooted in the social, legal and often fiscal systems of each country. Clearly some regulation is required to determine generally accepted methods of financial reporting but the means chosen for regulation has an important effect on the result.

In European countries, and to a lesser extent in other parts of the world, the basic rules for drawing up financial statements are specified in the law. Increasingly, however, it is being found that by itself the law is an awkward means of regulating accounting. In part this is because of the difficulty of changing the law, though secondary legislation may be used as a means of speeding up the process. The more fundamental reason, however, is that the subtle and continually developing demands of financial reporting nowadays make it necessary to give a fuller discussion of the accounting problem and its proposed solution than is possible in the narrow legalistic terms of statute. There are numerous examples of ingenious transactions that formally comply with the law while doing violence to its spirit. In principle, in EC Member states and certain other countries, such transactions could be dealt with by invoking the legal requirement that the financial statements should provide a "true and fair view" of the state of affairs of the enterprise and its profit or loss for the period. In practice, however, more detailed guidance than this is often needed in order to achieve comparable reporting by different enterprises.

These considerations have led many countries to establish accounting standards setting bodies either as quasi governmental committees or entirely within the private sector. These bodies act as a focus for public discussion on the most suitable way of developing generally accepted accounting practice and various means are found of effectively obtaining compliance with their pronouncements in the preparation of published financial statements.

Because accounting standards are reasoned and are issued only after a "due process" of public debate, they provide useful material for those in other countries who are investigating similar problems. There is a growing awareness of the need to work towards a greater comparability in financial reporting across the world. Through international meetings such as those sponsored by the OECD, through the continuing efforts of the International Accounting Standards Committee and through research by individual standards setting bodies a convergence of thinking is beginning to emerge on many accounting questions. The European Community has recently decided to encourage this process among its own Member states by creating an Accounting Consultative Forum that would examine common problems and attempt to find internationally acceptable solutions.

The exact form in which accounting problems arise and the possibilities for resolving them will often differ from country to country. There are, however, four broad sources of accounting complexity which are found to a greater or lesser extent in most countries and which constantly recur in the debates of standards setting bodies.

1) *Need for long-term estimates.* Problems arising in this area include: accounting for pension costs; making appropriate provision for an impairment in value of fixed assets; and determining period by period profit on long-term contracts.

2) *Instability in the financial environment.* Changes in the prices of an enterprise's assets, general inflation, changes in exchange rates and changes in interest rates can all radically alter the significance of accounting numbers. Views differ on the practicability of reflecting some or all of these effects in the financial statements.

3) *Innovations in commercial practice.* Sometimes innovatory transactions represent genuinely new ways of doing business; sometimes they seem more designed to influence the accounting than to affect the underlying commercial reality. In both cases such transactions challenge standards setters to re-consider and refine their principles to ensure that the financial statements present an adequate and not misleading picture of what has happened. Problems in this area include accounting for leases, new financial instruments (especially those that confuse the function of debt and equity) and "off-balance sheet finance".

4) *Presentational problems.* In addition to the above problems, which involve difficult questions of measurement and deciding whether an item should be included in the financial statements, there are a number of problems concerned with presentation, such as whether an item should be charged in arriving at operating profit, be shown as an extraordinary item or be charged to reserves.

In dealing with these and other problems that will emerge with the growing complexity of business, standards setting bodies and all concerned with accounting regulation should always seek solutions that will assist the presentation of "a true and fair view".

Information Needs of Users

Ingrid Scheibe-Lange

The main objective of financial statements in market economies is to provide useful information to users. Many conflicts in the accounting and reporting standard setting process can be explained by differing views on the question who the main user groups are and to what extent their information needs should be reflected.

This results in different answers to questions such as:

— Which types of enterprises should disclose financial reports (e.g. enterprises involved in financial market transactions, enterprises with limited liability, large-sized enterprises or all enterprises)?

— On which levels should disclosure be required (e.g. enterprise as a whole, individual member enterprise, subgroup, regional parts of a group, business line segments)?

— What type of information is to be provided?

— Which user groups should be included in the standard setting process?

An additional objective of financial statements is the determination of distributable profit. This usually applies to financial statements on the level of the individual enterprise and not on the level of the enterprise as a whole. Since accounting methods influence the volume of distributable profit as well as the information to be provided by the same financial statements, conflicts may arise between these two objectives. In some countries, financial accounts are used at the same time for taxation purposes. In such cases, the usefulness of these accounts to users is often much reduced.

The present status of national and international accounting and reporting standards in market economies can best be understood in the context of the historical process of developing such standards. During this process, views have changed concerning which user groups need to be informed on the performance and economic situation of an enterprise, and which type of information could and should meet their interests.

Investors

The need to protect investors has been recognised since the last century. This resulted in disclosure requirements for public limited liability enterprises. In some countries, such as the USA, investors (now including potential investors) are still the only user group whose information right is reflected by disclosure requirements. In such countries only public limited liability enterprises or enterprises whose securities are registered are obliged to

31

disclose accounts. The concept of information useful to meet investor needs has changed; from a focus on financial position and distributable profit to information about the past and present performance and its usefulness to evaluate future performance.

Creditors

Creditor protection has traditionally influenced accounting requirements. In some countries, a very conservative prudence concept was developed: it was felt that enterprises should be prevented from distributing too much to the shareholders, that it was sufficient to forbid overvaluation of assets, and that the creation of hidden reserves would not endanger the usefulness of such accounts. Today the dangers of hidden reserves are generally recognised: they can be secretly created as well as secretly dissolved in order to hide losses, and the profit trend as shown in the accounts is not the true one. From the creditor point of view, the future ability to generate profits and to repay debts is more important than the financial situation of the past. Nevertheless, in several countries it seems to be very difficult to change existing rules in order to apply such improved principles by forbidding hidden reserves.

The objective of creditor protection has more recently resulted in the requirement that all limited liability enterprises should disclose their financial statements. The EEC 4th and 7th Directives are good examples of this approach.

Other user groups

The standard setting process has recognised only lately the right of user groups other than investors and creditors to receive information on the performance and economic situation of enterprises. International frameworks now mention user groups such as present and potential investors, creditors, suppliers and customers, employees, governments and the public at large.

The main conflicts over which user groups' needs should be met by financial reports concern the employees, the general public and governments. It is often forgotten that in market economies as in centrally planned economies the main purpose of enterprises is not just to prosper on their own behalf but to contribute to the general welfare. The economic, social and environmental influences of enterprise on the local, national and international community are important factors and need to be monitored. Employees and their trade unions, for example, are interested in these macro-economic aspects of an enterprise's performance, as well as in its past and future financial stability and profitability and its social effects on employees within the enterprise, in particular with regard to wage payments, employment policy and working conditions.

Democracy and information

It is increasingly accepted that employees, the general public and governments are rightful users of financial reports. There is still debate as to the extent that their information needs should be met by financial statements. One conservative answer is: "only insofar as their needs are similar to the needs of other users such as investors and creditors". But this cannot be the final answer. Disclosure to the public is a means to monitor and control power in democratic societies. Information supplied to governments is by no means sufficient to satisfy the public interest, since governments represent political majorities, whereas all political parties and social interest groups must be able to get information in order to develop political programmes on all levels and use it in public discussions.

All enterprises of a certain importance, regardless of their legal form, should disclose financial reports, and these reports — in particular the notes to the accounts — need to reflect a broad range of the enterprise activities.

Governments and their agencies need information about the activities of enterprises for different purposes; for example, as a basis for national income and similar statistics, in order to monitor and regulate enterprise activities, and also as a basis for taxation. Taxation should preferably be based on special tax accounts that are independent from financial accounts. The experience in Western countries proves that wherever tax accounts and financial accounts are related, this results in disturbing some basic accounting and reporting concepts. For example, accelerated depreciation for tax purposes distorts income statement data and prevents a true and fair view of the enterprise. Tax considerations, an example being accounting for leasing, may also prevent the application of the important principle "substance over form".

More attention should be paid to the use of financial accounts as a basis for national statistics. This implies that the data derived from financial statements must be comparable with regard to their definition and valuation. Accounting standards that emphasis the concepts of flexibility and materiality may impair the comparability of information.

France, for example, supplements some of the principles mentioned above: all commercial enterprises have to disclose their financial accounts, the contents of these accounts are formalised to such an extent that they can be (and are) used as a basis for national statistics, and enterprises of a certain size have to disclose an additional social report ("bilan social").

Conclusion

The development and improvement of accounting and reporting standards is a political task, not a purely technical one. This implies that all main user groups should be involved in the standard setting process. The standards need to be backed by national law in order to ensure their application. Disclosure requirements should also ensure that financial reports are easily available, preferably at one central place in each country. All other forms of publication may in practice lead to non-availability.

Accounting in the Context of Transition to a Market Economy

Andrew Cunningham

The Soviet Union and the socialist countries of Central and Eastern Europe have all shared a similar approach to accounting. The methods adopted reflect the following key features:

— Budgeting and planning emanated from central control, and were only marginally influenced by managers of an enterprise;

— Production decisions followed closely from a central plan;

— Industry prices were established centrally, often to achieve a constant margin within an enterprise;

— Land was owned not by an enterprise but by the state itself; and, above all

— The concept of profit was of limited application, since it was beyond the control of management and could not thus be used in the measurement of performance.

In one respect, accounting was greatly simplified: accounting was essentially a statistical exercise, and comparability was of the essence. Thus all enterprises used the same accounts codes, and reported using identical forms. With the exception of banks, the sole user of financial information was the state. In the Polish context, a monthly summary profit and loss account was presented — principally to report turnover tax payable — and a balance sheet submitted annually. Separate forms were used to report production quantities, inventories and sales prices. Most importantly, financial statements were not presented to indicate a true and fair view to shareholders, and many of the accounting concepts developed internationally to reflect accruals, prudence and the substance of transactions had no application.

As far as the Soviet Union is concerned, it could be said that enterprises are, for accounting purposes, treated as "branches" of the Central Administration and, to that end, the chart of accounts sed by those enterprises provides information effectively detailing the utilisation of funds from the central administration, together with receipts from any other enterprises to whom it may sell goods or provides services. This means, in effect, that from an accounting point of view enterprises have, in the past, been responsible for reporting on the utilisation of funds placed with them from whatever source, rather than reporting on the "profitability" of any single venture. The central administration has had that responsibility if, indeed, profit has ever been a consideration in a centrally-controlled economy. Decisions of investment and profitability, together with other factors, may now be taken at local or individual enterprise level.

Today, change is being forced by the new entrants into the developing market economies, whether they be local or foreign entrepreneurs. Private business is allowed to compete on the same footing as state enterprise; and countries such as Poland, Czechoslovakia and Bulgaria allow 100 per cent foreign-owned companies to be created. Poland already has some 2 000 joint ventures since it passed its Foreign Investment Law in December 1988. Foreign investors wish to consolidate their new company's results into those of the parent at home, and need familiar management information to monitor their new investment.

At the same time, Hungary and Poland are undertaking the first privatisations of state enterprises, with provisions both for foreign investment and to encourage local individuals to acquire a stake. Foreign banks are arriving and requesting financial information to assess a loan application. The larger state enterprises are realising that, to maintain their dominance, they must attract new capital and present their profile. And, last but not least, governments themselves are in need of realistic financial statements which identify those enterprises unable to survive, without guaranteed sales prices and subsidies. All of the new users demand financial statements which enable them to monitor and assess the health of their investments.

The first-time investor visiting a potential partner in Eastern Europe will be presented with a set of financial statements. Assuming that he can read them, a number of conceptual difficulties will need to be overcome — and all will need to be tackled on a wider scale if accountants from West and East are to understand each other in future. He is likely to find property stated at a centrally determined valuation — Poland increased book values by a factor of 11 to 15 on 1st January 1990, for example, to keep pace with inflation — and depreciation over a much longer period than he is used to. Due to a need to reflect central prices, stock may be carried at a standard cost. Provisions for bad debts, which may today be critical feature is unlikely to be prudent, based rather on administrative decisions then management assessment.

Accruals will have been made for physical goods received into stock, but almost certainly not for overheads. He will not find a statement of accounting policies, since these result from central accounting regulations; nor will he find reference to guarantees or other contingent liabilities on the one hand and funds representing ownership or special purposes on the other; indeed the concept of a social or housing fund for employees may baffle a person used only to share capital and reserves. He will look at the profit and loss account and find no provision for corporate income tax and other payments due to the state. And finally, how will he attempt to assess profitability when the enterprise may be facing rampant inflation? Current cost accounting is no more popular in Eastern Europe than in the West.

All these issues must be faced if companies and enterprises in Eastern Europe are to attract outside interest and investment, and if the countries themselves are to find a welcome in the European Community. But there are no ready solutions which can be forced upon Poland, Hungary or their neighbours by the accounting bodies of the West. It is worth remembering that, despite the upheavals of the past year, the state still accounts for at least 85 per cent of GNP in most of the countries in transition.

The only realistic solutions are those which recognise the particular circumstances of each country in Central and Eastern Europe and are carefully developed to meet those circumstances. Until the market economy is fully up and running, adapting, rather than replacing, the present accounting systems must surely be the objective.

Accounting Issues Arising in the Context of the Transition to Market Economies: The Experience of Poland

Alicja Jaruga

Transition from a centrally planned economy to a market economy is an extremely complicated process. The system of ownership is changing, while the market does not yet function. A move away from the practice of keeping artificial prices, as well as their relation to real prices, is taking place. All this is happening after a period of hyperinflation in Poland. Internal convertibility of national currency has been realised. Governmental subsidies have been eliminated or considerably limited. These are only examples of economic and institutional changes towards commercialisation, corporatisation and privatisation.

Had these changes taken place gradually, the adaptation of accountancy and its underlying legal basis would have been easier. As these changes affect the restatement and revaluation adjustments in financial statements of enterprises, as well as valuation of an entity, the whole process is very complicated.

In elaborating new accounting and reporting regulations we should take into consideration, on the one hand, the enterprise continuing its activities in the long run, and on the other hand, those concepts which are strictly connected with transforming the going concern through privatisation and mergers. The first issue requires a new legal structure whereas the latter is very difficult to determine without the existence of a capital market. The basic concepts of financial statements should be distinguished from those concepts relating to bankruptcy, take-over, or change in the form of ownership, etc. This also requires an adequate legal structure.

In a centrally planned economy the aggregation of data for statistical and planning purposes and financial control required a very high degree of standardisation of accounting and unification of financial statements. The latter were imposed by statistical requirements such as the formula for estimating the net national income.

In market economies, providing information on business activities to facilitate decision making by external and internal users is a fundamental objective, whereas in centrally planned economies controlling functions are the most important. Thus different economic structures served different needs of users.

Financial accounting as a part of the economic information system, and financial statements of enterprises are primarily addressed to governmental authorities. In this context, book-keeping rules are laid down in detailed regulations for every kind of business transaction. At the same time, principal concepts were frequently not articulated, and sometimes were treated instrumentally, and were accommodated to the needs of economic practice.

Transition from centrally planned economies towards a market system calls for appropriate changes in accounting regulations. Commercialised and private enterprises, and joint ventures must function in commercial conditions. New economic information users require information on the financial position and performance of an enterprise. Hence, an urgent need exists for new accounting regulations in Central and Eastern European countries exists, which would reflect the needs of all main users: managers, investors, creditors, government, etc. Such regulations must take into account both concepts and the principles of accountancy applied in market economies, and the accumulated experiences with these concepts and principles.

It is essential to select the accounting system best suited for application in a given country. The EC Directives (4th, 7th) which accept the lowest common denominator between several nations with regard to accounting requirements, seem to be the most appropriate. It is also possible to benefit from the experience of other OECD Member countries. The French General Accounting Plan provides the structure for adapting Polish accounting to the requirements of a market economy. However, this structure can be supplemented by accounting practices of other West European countries which meet the present needs of the Polish economy (eg. the conduct of auditing in achieving accountability in Britain).

Another question concerning the choice of an appropriate system is whether the International Accounting Standards (IAS) are complementary to the EC Directives. The need to attract foreign capital to the countries of Central and Eastern Europe requires that the IAS be adopted so as to increase investors' confidence. In Poland, a group of accounting professionals advocate the adoption of the IAS. Another group is of the opinion that IAS can only be adopted if they are consistent with the implementation of the EC Directives.

The objective of accounting reforms in Poland and Hungary is to improve the understanding and practice of accounting leading to increased economic efficiency. The transition from a centrally planned economy to a market system also affects accounting and reporting concepts and principles formerly designed for planning, monitoring, and administrative control:

The entity concept, nominally functioned as an accounting, and not business entity concept, because there existed no clear and full distinction between state-owned enterprises and the owner in the centrally planned economy, i.e. so-called full economic accountability was only imitated.

The going - concern concept could not be applied since state-owned enterprises had no, or very little, influence upon development, growth and reinvestment. Accumulation funds were collected centrally. Enterprises running a loss were compensated by means of subsidies.

The accrual concept has been generally applied by state-owned enterprises in Hungary, Czechoslovakia, and Poland (with some modifications in 1986-1988).

The concept of prudence was limited to inventories valuation according to "lower cost or market"; it is recently applied in Poland more widely.

The substance over legal form principle has not yet been introduced.

The historical cost principle is common practice in centrally planned economies (with the exception of hyperinflation countries).

The consistency principle of book-keeping has long been applied.

The structure of the balance sheet and income statement is undergoing serious transformations in order to meet the objectives of accounting in market economies (as of 1.1.1991). Formerly, the balance sheet primarily indicated whether financial rules were being followed, whereas, at present, it is closer to the EC Directives. Goodwill and other intangible assets have been introduced; equity and long-term debts have been clearly distinguished.

Adapting accounting regulations to a market economy necessitates settling the question of the purpose of financial statements and underlying principles; whether it is to evaluate the past for fiscal requirements, or to help in future decision-making. In Poland, the second approach has been chosen.

Although there is a need for a drastic reduction of governmental regulations and rules concerning accounting and financial reporting the transition period requires a certain degree of governmental regulations based on legal acts. A uniform, chart of accounts, designed under a micro-economic approach is expected to be an appropriate aid for incorporating the new governmental regulations.

Forty years of separation of Central and East European countries (and over seventy years in the Soviet Union) has resulted in a gap in the terminology used in accountancy. In the course of translating EC Directives, IAS, Conceptual Framework (IASC and FASB), and other basic regulations and standards of accounting, frequent use is made of many foreign textbooks (English, French, and German) in order to properly render the meaning and spirit of some terms and concepts, (eg. "true and fair view", "contingencies", "hedges"). It is still difficult to be sure of the right interpretation of these terms in practice.

The EC Directives (4th, 7th, 8th), IAS and the first lexicon of accounting in Polish will soon be published sponsored by the Accountants Association in Poland. The OECD and FEE will be instrumental in assisting the transition efforts of the formally centralised economies to market systems.

Current Accounting Problems in the Former GDR

Dietz Mertin

The great number of daily publications on latest developments in Eastern Europe have made more than clear the complexity and difficulty of converting a centrally planned economy into a market economy. The accountant may now prove his skill — at least as far as East Germany is concerned — by presenting this transition in a true and fair manner and in such a way that the newly established companies will not suffer on over-indebtedness right away.

On July 1, 1990 the Deutsche Mark was introduced in East Germany. The Agreement on Currency, Economic and Social Union provides for a conversion rate for receivables and payables of 2 East Marks for 1 Deutsche Mark. It was impossible to fix any rates for other assets and accruals because the accounting system in East Germany had been totally different from that in Western industrialised countries.

The State Treaty further required the passing of a law in East Germany on the preparation of opening balance sheets in Deutsche Mark and reassessment of capital which will apply to all businessmen and legal entities including combines (Kombinate) and companies owned by the people (volkseigene Betriebe). For the opening balance sheet, the State Treaty requires the following principles to be included in the law on the preparation of opening balance sheets:

1) Assets and liabilities must be reassessed.

2) Assets are to be stated at their depreciated replacement cost, taking into account technological progress. Self-produced intangible assets are not allowed to be capitalised.

3) Any excess of liabilities over assets is capitalised as an equalisation claim to avoid over-indebtedness. Such equalisation claim is subject to approval by the Federal government.

4) In other respects the accounting principles of the West German Commercial Code apply.

The foregoing basic principles are intended to guarantee that assets are not overvalued and debts are not undervalued at the expense of investors and creditors.

The *Treuhandanstalt,* a government authority which acted formerly as administrator of state-owned property, was newly established as the holding company of all East German state-owned enterprises with the aim of restructuring and transforming these enterprises into stock corporations and limited liability companies and to sell their shares to private investors.

Besides the purely technical accounting issues, there are other problems which stem from the former centrally planned economy and from political circumstances. These are:

1) The centrally planned economy's aim was fulfilment of the plan and not generation of profits. Equity capital was of lesser importance. Assets allocated by the government were balanced with equal amounts of liabilities or funds.

   Annual revaluation by government led to considerable over-valuation of assets. Accruals were only allowed to a limited extend. Payments to meet environmental protection obligations or social plan costs for necessary dismissals were not recorded and cannot yet be estimated.

2) Legal uncertainty is wide-spread, in particular as regards acquiring property, because ownership rights are not yet clarified.

3) Although the above mentioned laws and measures are designed to enhance investment, investors are presently still reluctant. This is also due to uncertain wage policies; wage settlements also must be more production-oriented.

4) There is a lack of knowledge in planning and organisation, management and marketing techniques, as well as in costing methods.

5) Products are partly not competitive, e.g. East German cars will, if at all, be exported to some east european countries, but can no longer be sold in Germany. Obsolete production plants and technological backwardness, environmental problems, inflated administrations and excessive workforce- are all significant problems affecting accounting and valuation in the Deutsche Mark opening balance sheet.

As concerns balance sheet items in particular:

— Real estate: the so-called market value as provided in the State Treaty does not yet exist for the time being. In the meantime, West German real estate prices may be taken as a basis for valuation.

— Deferred maintenance and repairs not carried out for decades will be an important component in the valuation of buildings.

— It is questioned whether a large number of machines and technical equipment can still be used for business purposes because companies have to try to adjust their product range to market requirements. In cases where machines have been imported, there is often a particular need for depreciation due to the former state credit system, adverse exchange rates and the annual price level adjustment for assets by the former GDR government.

— Particular treatment will be applied to the valuation of capital investment now being established through privatisation by the *Treuhandanstalt*. At present, there are neither acquisition costs nor market values. The equity method will be used in order to determine the value to be included in the opening balance sheet. However, in future years, such opening balance sheet value will be treated as acquisition cost and the equity method abandoned because it is not admitted as an accounting principle in Germany according to the EC Fourth Directive.

— As already mentioned, the Deutsche Mark opening balance sheet will reflect considerably more accruals e.g. for social reasons due to necessary dismissals.

Because of the difficulty of finding the right value for all assets and liabilities prior to the functioning of a market economy, correction of first year valuation will be allowed until 1994. Such adjustments will appear on the income statement and will be taxable.

Considering all these valuation problems it is clear that over-indebtedness and going-concern are the crucial problems to be solved.

The approach to avoid over-indebtedness is scheduled in three consecutive steps:

As a first step, over-indebtedness will be balanced by an equalisation claim against *Treuhandanstalt*. Conversely a "debt rescheduling" leads to a liability to *Treuhandanstalt*. *Treuhandanstalt* may only accept the equalisation claim if the enterprise can remain a going-concern.

Secondly, if and when the equalisation claim against *Treuhandanstalt* has been admitted because the company is regarded as a going-concern, then the enterprise will be allowed to set up the legal minimum share capital. The equivalent on the asset side is recorded as "capital contribution outstanding".

Thirdly, those enterprises with the required minimum capital may set up "preliminary revenue reserves", and equivalent asset item, e.g. in respect of self-generated intangible assets. This is, however, subject to the reasonable assumption that the enterprise will be able to earn the depreciation on such asset item over the following four years.

The Modernisation of the Hungarian Accounting System

Mrs. Maria Dudàs

In recent years, Hungary has made significant progress in the process of the establishment of a market economy. The objective of the Government's economic policy is to establish a liberalised market economy integrated into the world market, where private ownership plays a decisive role. In this context, the present accounting system, which evolved under the conditions of the command economy must now be revised.

The modernisation of the accounting system began simultaneously with the modernisation of the system of taxation. The changes implemented over the past few years have begun to close the gap between Hungarian and international accounting practices.

One of the most frequently cited problems of the present accounting system is that its primary objective is to serve the information needs of a central economic control. As a result balance sheet reporting requirements place a heavy burden on the enterprise to supply information which does not serve the needs of the enterprises nor the interests of their clients.

The utilisation of accounting information as the fundamental basis of national economic information has created a strict and detailed regulatory framework. The highly complicated nature of this accounting system was further aggravated by its close linkage to taxation.

In the course of recent transformation of state enterprises the accuracy of the value of assets as stated by the accounting system has been questioned in many cases although the main reason behind this is not due to the accounting system.

The system of accounting and the regulations pertaining thereto are closely related to the economy of a country and its system of control. In Hungary, the present system of accounting evolved after World War II under the conditions of the command economy. During the period of highly centralized economic control (1950-1954), the tasks of accounting were to measure and control the fulfillment of the plans and to provide inventories and recording of the means of production owned by the state.

Following the introduction of the system of profit incentives (1955-1967), the tasks of accounting were extended to cover the facilitation of savings, the monitoring of the development of prime costs and the measurement of the reduction of prime costs.

The development of the present uniform system of accounting was linked to the introduction of the economic reforms of 1968 and was implemented in several stages (1971, 1976, 1983, 1988).

47

Accounting provided the functional bodies of economic control (National Planning Office, Ministry of Finance, National Bank of Hungary, Central statistics Office) and through them, the Government, with the information necessary for making economic decisions.

The identity of accounting and statistical terms (their homogeneity of content), the harmonisation of the methods of calculation of factors such as production value, value added and other parameters enabled the Central Statistics office to use the globalised data of the balance sheet reports of the enterprises for the calculation of the social product, national income, GDP, etc.

The balance sheet reporting system also provides the Ministry of Finance with information on the functioning of prevailing income regulations, and the system of taxation, as well as a basis for planning public expenditures.

Strict and detailed state regulations continue to apply to all of accounting and its sub-areas, these regulations are, particularly in recent times, regarded as highly excessive by the economic organisations. The basic accounting regulation was the Act on State Finances; its Chapter 9 contains the regulations pertaining to the system of accounting information. In accordance with that law, decrees of the Minister of Finance regulate the obligation to prepare a balance sheet and an income statement, their formats, the method of valuing the items of the balance sheet, the content of the Uniform National Economic Chart of Accounts supporting these, the decimal system of accounts and the method of keeping them. In order to protect state property, the regulations also covered inventories, prime costing, the order of documentation as well as the order of handling cash.

This comprehensive state regulation applying to all areas of accounting also provides a reliable foundation for the financial audits carried out by the tax authorities.

The regulations pertaining to the determination of the activities of economic organisations was particularly strict. Neither the Act on Corporate Profit Taxation, nor the accounting regulation permit the assertion of business considerations, as that would provide an opportunity for drawing certain items out of the sphere of taxation, eventually even for tax fraud.

In view of the fact that Hungary has made significant progress in the establishment of a market economy and that various measures attempt to create a favorable economic environment for foreign investors, the two basic functions of accounting, namely, the supply of information necessary for decision making by the government and serving the taxation system, cannot remain unchanged in this changing environment.

Modernisation of accounting is a priority, primarily in order that accountants obtain the knowledge accumulated in countries with market economies with which they will be able to contribute to the successful implementation of the privatisation process and to take part in the development of business strategies in an efficient manner. The establishment of an accounting system that will meet the information needs of the market agents (entrepreneurs, investors, creditors) is an integral part of the process of market building. The legal basis of the new system will be created by the accounting law.

Both domestic and foreign investors urge a transformation of accounting regulations whereby information giving a true and fair view of the net assets, financial and income position of the enterprises in line with international accounting principles and accepted practices, would be made available to those concerned. Therefore legal regulations focus on the determination of the content of the annual financial report incorporating the accounting information, its auditing by independent auditors and its disclosure.

That is to say, the emphasis of accounting regulation is being shifted to the "substantial"; the philosophy of regularity is being replaced by that of the "true and fair view". The strict and detailed state regulations pertaining to accounting and all its areas is being replaced by a flexibly implementable regulation that will render the development of an enterprise-friendly accounting possible.

Those preparing the annual financial report will be liable, after the promulgation of the new Act, not for compliance with the detailed rules of bookkeeping, but for true content of the financial report prepared in accordance with the internationally accepted accounting principles, for the reality of the result and net assets presented therein.

State regulation implemented with the enactment of the new law will assume a new type of entrepreneurial approach that will enable entrepreneurs to develop their own accounting policies and their assertion from the point of view of the "prudent businessman".

In practice, the financial report based on the provisions of the law will have to be "true and fair" according to the terminology applied in the countries of the European Community, or "fairly established" as it is said in the United States. This strengthens confidence in the accounting system, since the final reports satisfy international expectations, they will be directly comparable with the financial reports of the EEC countries.

The law is based on internationally accepted accounting principles, most of which had already been incorporated in the earlier accounting regulations. As long as the principle of going concern can be applied to the enterprise. the assets of the enterprise are to be valued at historical (purchase, production) value. Valuing at market value becomes predominant only when the enterprise cannot continue to operate.

The principle of prudence appeared in the Hungarian accounting system only as concerns lower of cost. This is the principle that renders accounting enterprise-friendly. It prevents the presentation of non-realized profits, that is, the result cannot be shown if the financial realisation of any revenue becomes uncertain irrespective of performance (the delivery of goods or the performance of services). It also follows from the principle of prudence that all foreseeable risks and expected losses must be taken into account as items reducing the result, even if such facts become known during the period between the accounting date and the preparation of the balance sheet.

In addition to the net assets and the financial an income position of the enterprise the financial report will provide, the creditor and the investor with information on how the current year developed, and the viability and credit worthiness of the enterprise.

The accounting law will also require auditing by an independent auditor and disclosure.

Main Elements of Financial Reporting

The Legal Infrastructure of Accounting and Reporting

Karel van Hulle

Introduction

No society can function without a legal infrastructure which organises human relations. In a modern society, this legal infrastructure has become increasingly complex. This is no doubt also the case in the business environment. As accounting is the reflection of business reality, accounting is also heavily influenced by the legal infrastructure. Before a business transaction can be recorded in the accounts, it will often be necessary to examine the legal nature of the transaction. This is the reason why in different countries similar transactions can be subject to a different accounting treatment because the legal nature of the transaction may be different. On the other hand, in most OECD countries it is now recognised that the accounts must show a true and fair view and that the form of a transaction must not be dissociated with its substance.

Differences in the legal environment reflect different choices based upon different priorities. These choices are the result of historical developments, of cultural heritage and tradition. These differences affect the relative importance given to accounting and financial reporting as well as the structure of the accounting standard setting process. As a result of a survey conducted by the OECD Working Group on Accounting Standards in 1978/1979, three main approaches to the way standards are established and implemented in Member countries were identified. The first one is of a legal nature where accounting practices are governed by laws and regulations. This was the method prevailing in the EC as well as in some other European countries. The second approach is based on self-regulation by the accounting profession, in some cases in conjunction with the business community and other groups interested in accounting. This was the method identified predominantly in the US, Canada, Australia and New Zealand and to some extent also in Ireland and in the UK. The third approach, which being primarily of legal character, relies to a large extent on consultation between public authorities and accounting standard setting bodies in which a broad range of interests are represented. France, Belgium, the Netherlands, Spain and Japan were identified as examples

In the accounting literature, different models have been developed to classify the various accounting systems. The advantage of such classifications is that they help to understand the differences between the accounting systems of different countries. The disadvantage is that these classifications are an oversimplification of a sometimes complex reality and that these classifications tend to overlook hidden similarities.

Because of the internationalisation of business and of the capital markets, the need for comparability of financial information has increased over the last years. In this context, the question arises whether it will be possible to develop a set of accounting standards which can be used by companies operating in an international environment and to what extent this international framework will affect the local infrastructure of accounting and financial reporting. It is not possible to understand financial statements without some understanding about the socio-economic, the cultural and the legal environment from which these financial statements originate.

Accounting and company law

Not so long ago, the permission to carry out a corporate activity was granted by government charter or by parliament. Governments were suspicious about the creation of corporate ghosts having a separate legal personality. As a matter of fact, the assets brought into the corporation do not belong anymore to its former owners but become the property of the legal person.

In some countries, the permission to carry out a corporate activity under the legal form of a company with separate legal personality was conditioned upon the publication by that legal person of financial information. Disclosure of financial information was felt necessary in order to make the legal person accountable towards its shareholders, the government, creditors and the public at large.

In the EC but also in other European countries, this tradition has brought about the rule that all limited liability companies have to publish financial information. This rule is justified by the fact that special protection should be given to shareholders and third parties because of the limited liability of the company. The accounts published by the company had to be audited first by a representative of the shareholders and later by a professional accountant.

Meanwhile, some countries have gone beyond this stage and require all large undertakings (even if they are not limited liability companies) to disclose financial information. The justification of this rule is the economic importance of this undertaking and its relevance for the socio-economic environment.

The company law approach in accounting and financial reporting has influenced the nature of a number of accounting rules. This is very apparent in the EC accounting directives. To mention a few examples: the legal capital maintenance concept (the capital which is the ultimate guarantee for creditors may not be impaired by any form of distribution which does not find its origin in profits generated by the company); the importance given to the balance sheet as opposed to the profit and loss account.

Accounting and capital markets

Investor protection has been the primary objective of accounting regulation in a number of OECD countries. The requirement to disclose financial information is imposed upon all entities having made a public issue of securities or whose securities have been listed on a stock exchange.

The information to be disclosed must be *timely* (including intra-annual financial information) and is geared towards the actual and potential investors. In this context, the profit and loss account is considered to be more important than the balance sheet and accounting rules have been developed allowing companies to accelerate the recording of profits.

The information which is disclosed will normally also be subject to an audit requirement.

Accounting and taxation

In all OECD countries, a large part of the state budget is financed by taxation levied upon the profits realised by business undertakings. It is therefore logical, that States have shown a keen interest in the way businesses have defined their taxable profits.

In some OECD countries, there is an identity or a close linkage between the financial information produced in general purpose reports and the financial information which is produced for tax purposes. In those countries tax legislation and accounting legislation are very closely linked.

In other OECD countries, there is a separation between the financial information produced in general purpose reports and the financial information which is produced for tax purposes.

However, in reality the situation is not always very clear. It is fair to say that in all OECD countries tax law has an important impact on the ways and means business is conducted. Because accounting is the reflection of that business reality, accounting is bound to be influenced by tax considerations.

On the other hand, where there is a close linkage between accounting and taxation, financial information is heavily influenced by tax strategy. This will sometimes result in an overemphasis of the prudence principle in order to postpone the tax burden as long as possible.

In the EC where both approaches exist, the accounting Directive allows the accounts to be coloured by tax valuations on the condition that the effects of such valuation are indicated in the notes to the accounts.

Nature of accounting standards

In some OECD Member countries, accounting standards are part of the law (company law). This is notably the case in all EC Member States as a result of the accounting harmonisation process which requires Member States to incorporate the provisions of the accounting directives into national law. In this case, the enforcement of the accounting standards takes place through the normal mechanisms of the law. In some EC Member States the accounting law is supplemented by standards issued by a standard setting body, which may be a professional body or a body which includes representatives of the profession, the various groups of users and preparers and interested government agencies. The legal status of such standards is not always clear. There is however a growing tendency to give these standards also legal backing.

In other OECD Member countries, the profession has a predominant influence on standard setting. This is most clearly the case in the US, Canada, Australia, and New Zealand. Although the legal situation in these countries is not exactly the same, the law may require financial statements to be prepared in accordance with the standards adopted by a professional standard setting body or the standard setting may be delegated by a government agency to a professional standard setting body. Where the accounting profession plays an important role in setting the standards, disciplinary rules are there to ensure that members of the profession respect these standards.

Conclusion

Law plays an important role in accounting and financial reporting. This fact must be reflected in the education and training of the accounting profession. The degree of importance may differ from country to country and there is sometimes a communication gap between accountants and lawyers, but the fact remains that it is impossible to understand the financial statements without some understanding of the legal and indeed socio-economic environment in which these statements originate. The relative importance of these considerations varies from country to country but they do have an influence on the nature of the information which is required to be published as well as on the way the accounting legislation is being structured.

Balance Sheet Layout and Valuation Principles

Veijo Riistama

Axioms of financial accounting

Because accounting belongs to "sciences of artificial" we need a set of axioms to be able to present any comprehensive approach on accounting. Usually we rely on generally accepted accounting principles. They are, however, not very exact and can be interpreted in many ways. They may even appear contradictory, e.g. the principles of matching and prudence.

To understand balance sheet layout and valuation principles, one has to have a comprehensive picture of accounting. According to the diagram below, financial accounting can be considered to be a description of the monetary process (flows) of a firm (or any other entity). There are two processes in a firm: the production process and the monetary process. The former one is reflected in the latter one.

A firm is surrounded by three markets: production factors, sales and financial markets. It has two sources of money: capital and revenue. Expenses, distribution of income and repayment of capital are three uses of money.

All the relevant implications can be derived from this basic conceptual approach on accounting. The basic axioms are:

— Financial accounting is a description of monetary flows of an economic entity.

— Book-keeping is recording of three types of transactions: revenues, expenses and monetary transactions, as well as their corrective items.

— Over the entire life time of the enterprise, the total profit recorded equals the total cash flows generated as a difference between revenues and expenses.

— Assets are measured according to the cash paid in acquiring them, that is, historical cost is the valuation basis in the books.

— Recording of revenues and expenses is based on realisation principle. Realisation takes place whenever a product or service is delivered or procured. In many cases, delivery does not mean change of legal ownership but change of economic ownership. The interpretation and application of realisation principle depends very much on the social and legal environment.

- Before preparing annual accounts all the revenues and expenses are recognised and recorded according to the accrual principle.
- Allocating the effects of transactions between periods for reporting purposes is the most important question in preparing the annual accounts. In every annual report it is necessary to divide expenses into two categories: those which have already contributed to revenues, or for which no revenue is any more expected, and those which are expected to contribute to future revenues. The former ones are matched with the revenues of the accounting period. The latter ones are deferred (under the name of assets) to future periods to be matched with the respective revenues. The difference between revenues and expenses in the income statement is profit or loss.

In solving the problems of allocating the effects of transactions between accounting periods, we need two generally accepted accounting principles: accruals and prudence — however conflicting they may sometimes be. The underlying principle is matching, although in practice it has to give way to the principle of prudence.

Preparing the annual accounts

Preparation of annual accounts means:
- Recognising all revenues and expenses on an accrual basis;
- Dividing expenses into two: those which have contributed to revenues or are no more expected to contribute to them (e.g. purchase value of goods sold or spoiled, depreciation), and those which are expected to contribute to revenues in the future;
- Dividing revenues into two: one part covering the expenses, the other part being profit or loss. Loss means that an unsuccessful attempt has been made to cover realised expenses by realised revenues;
- Presenting the balances on the accounts in the balance sheet.

Technically, it is not necessary to prepare a balance sheet. Congruent book-keeping could be continued without any balance sheet preparation.

Balance sheet layout

The basic structure of a balance sheet is as follows:

Balance Sheet

Cash and similar monatary items	Liabilities
	- Short term
	- Long term
	(Revaluation items)
Deferred expenses	
- Current	Provisions
- Fixed	
	Equity
(Revaluation items)	

A non-monetary asset is nothing else but an expense incurred before the balance sheet date and, on an accruals basis, is expected to contribute to revenues beyond the balance sheet date. This approach covers also immaterial current and fixed assets: examples are deferred expenses of unfinished planning or computer programming works in current assets and deferred expenses of development projects in fixed assets.

This approach puts the primary emphasis on preparing the profit and loss statement. The balance sheet can be seen also as a mere collection of monetary assets, liabilities and equity, and what is left over after presenting revenues and costs in the income statement. As a matter of fact it is the earning power of the firm, its ability to generate income which is the most important and interesting feature of a firm evaluated in the financial market.

Nowadays the earning power of a firm is, in many cases, more due to immaterial than material assets. Skilful personnel, know-how and good marketing channels are examples of "assets" which do not appear in the balance sheet figures. Information concerning these factors belongs either in the annual report or in notes to the accounts. They are reflected anyhow in the figures of the income statement.

Valuation principles

The basic valuation principle of assets in a going concern is historical cost subject to the need of write downs in anticipation of losses. Many of the problems called valuation problems are, as a matter of fact, problems of matching. Valuation of inventories (stock) and fixed assets are examples of those problems. This applies to immaterial fixed assets, like development costs.

There are, however, lots of "genuine" valuation problems to be solved. Examples are:

— Problems due to foreign currency translation,

— Applying mark-to-market principle to monetary items, and

— Valuation problem in cases where there is an exchange of commodities between firms without any monetary transaction.

Transforming a previously centralised economy into a market economy presents a special valuation problem. Some value must be attached to the production facilities previously owned by the state in and transferred to the newly established firms. There is seldom an opportunity to find any unanimous market value, or "arm's length value", which would easily solve the problem.

The basis for the valuation problems is, according to the accounting approach described above, expectations. The principle of prudence must be followed with regard to these expectations. Actually, it is not possible to prepare a balance sheet (and income statement) without taking the future into consideration. Expectations are a starting point for matching investment expenses against revenues (depreciation), for estimating credit losses, for evaluating receivables and liabilities in foreign currency, as well as for anticipating the development of the market value of a financial instrument.

There are very few operational methods available when it comes to the valuation of production facilities transferred to newly established firms in previously centralised economies. In the absence of market prices, the best possible theoretical value must be based on the discounted future cash flow of the firm in question. In many cases, transfers concern whole plants and factories. There are two sides to the coin in these cases: the higher the value, the better the solidity of the firm acquiring them. On the other hand: the higher the value, the higher will the future depreciation and comparable cost be (this may not be critical in case of land and other non-depreciable assets).

Income Statements and Profit Allocation

Herman Marseille

Introduction

The Framework for the Preparation and Presentation of Financial Statements of the IASC (International Accounting Standards Committee) provides a useful basis for the subject of this paper. The main elements of this framework are presented in a table at the end of this article.

Companies operating in market economies deal with uncertainties reflecting the volatility and dynamics of these economies. Changes in the volume- and price potentials of a certain market and changes in competition continually take place. The extent to which those aspects effect the performance of a company depends on the capability of a company to respond to the inherent challenges and risks.

In a market economy, the performance, as shown in the annual accounts, should reflect the capabilities of a company — i.e. its ability to satisfy the needs of customers at a competitive cost and by innovating its products and services regularly. Financial reports provide users, like financial analysts, with vital data for the assessment of the quality of business entities and their earning capacity, particularly when these reports are comparable with those of preceding years and with performance records of competitors.

Although local regulations and, consequently, local accounting practices differ from country to country, there is less difference of opinion on the basic assumptions underlying the preparation and presentation of financial statements of which the income statement forms a part. This paper focuses mainly on these general principles.

In the major industrial countries, the measurement of performance results from the application of the historical cost model and from using the financial concept of capital. These principles imply that profit is measured as the positive difference between realised income and related expenses based on historical cost, the last irrespective of intermediary price increases including those related to decreasing purchasing power of the reporting currency.

An underlying assumption is that financial statements are prepared on the accrual basis of accounting. "Under this basis, the effects of transactions and other events are recognised when they occur (and not as cash or its equivalent is received or paid) and they are recorded in the accounting records and reported in the financial statements of the periods to which they relate." (IASC Framework Par 22). Accrual accounting is applied by the business community in market economies and is clearly distinctive from cash-accounting.

Standards for the measurement of performance

General

Performance is measured primarily by allocating the revenues to which the company is entitled to the reporting periods to which they relate (realisation principle, revenue recognition) and, subsequently, by allocating the expenses related to these revenues to the same period (matching concept). Those two principles are the main concepts for the measurement of performance.

Both the realisation principle and the matching concept are supplemented by the requirement that interperiod allocation of (expected) cashflows do result in "transfer" amounts in the balance sheet (either debits or credits) which satisfy the definitions and the recognition criteria for assets and liabilities.

Although not always stated explicitly, it is believed that income and expenses should be comprehended fully in the calculation of performance (all-inclusive concept).

Revenue recognition

IAS 18 requires recognition when:
— The seller of the goods has transferred to the buyer the significant risks and rewards of ownership, in that all significant acts have been completed and the seller retains no continuing managerial involvement in, or effective control of, the goods transferred to a degree usually associated with ownership; and
— No significant uncertainty exist regarding:
  i) The consideration that will be derived from the sale of the goods;
  ii) The associated costs incurred or to be incurred in producing or purchasing the goods;
  iii) The extent to which goods may be returned.

These criteria for sales of goods follow from the consideration that reliability of measurement is a fundamental quality element of financial statements. Only when ultimate collection can reasonably be expected can sales be, and should be, recognised. Delivering the goods sold to the customers is usually understood as meeting these criteria.

The same is true for services. In the case of long-term service contracts, revenues are measured according to either the percentage of completion method or the completed contract method. The recently issued Statement of Intent of IASC states that the methods no longer should be optional: when the outcome of the contract can be reliably estimated, revenue should be recognised by reference to the stage of completion (percentage of completion method), in other cases only to the extent that costs are incurred and can be recovered (profit then will be recognised according to the completed contract method).

These rules also apply to construction contracts. In many countries, the completed contract method is the preferred, or required, method of accounting for construction contracts. Some believe, as IASC does, that the percentage of completion method provides the most relevant information to users if the recognition criteria are met. Others attach more weight to the reliability of information and favour the completed contract method; they believe that prudence should lead to the recognition of profits not earlier than at final delivery.

The tests for recognition of revenues generally are applied on an item by item basis, rather than on a portfolio basis, for groups of homogeneous transactions. However, uncertainty with respect to the ultimate collection of a specific receivable arising from a sales transaction, for example, should not necessarily lead to non-recognition. Statistical records might show the extent to which ultimate collection from similar transactions can be expected. Probability and measurability usually are positively effected by greater numbers of similar transactions.

The matching concept

Expenses are allocated to the same periods in which the related revenues are recognised. This matching concept applies to expenses which are both directly and indirectly related to revenues. IAS 2 (Accounting for Inventories) states that cost of manufactured inventories should include those production overhead costs that relate to putting the inventories in their present location and condition. By absorbing these costs in inventories they are matched with the revenues in the period of sale ("product-matching").

Expenses which are only remotely related to revenues (or not at all) are recognised in the period they occur ("period-matching").

Accounting for hedge transactions is a form of matching. A hedge transaction can be defined as a transaction by which a certain position with inherent risk — for instance a currency risk — is covered. The risk element of both the hedged transaction or hedged position and the hedge transaction should be dealt with consistently.

The asset/liability test

Both revenue-recognition and matching are the main concepts for the calculation of net income. They determine profit on the basis of historical cost at its own right. The asset/liability-test follows from the consistency of balance sheet and income statement and from the definitions of income and expenses set out in the IASC Framework. According to the Board of IASC, the asset/liability-test does not affect the evenhanded approach to balance sheet and income statement as income only will be generated if resulting in increases of assets or decreases of liabilities.

Usually the asset/liability-test does not conflict with the profit-concept on the basis of both revenue recognition and matching principle. The treatment of research and development costs might illustrate that a pure income/expense approach — with its emphasis on matching — might conflict with a pure balance sheet approach — with a natural emphasis on prudence. Market and industrial know-how are prerequisites for an ongoing existence of companies in a market economy. Companies therefore spend substantial resources to maintain their know-how and their positions in the market. Matching in a strict sense means that these expenses, if they can be identified separately, are set off against future revenues. However, deferred charges, although satisfying the definition of assets frequently do not meet the recognition tests and, in that case, should not be included in the balance sheet. In many instances, it follows, such research and development costs have to be expensed in the periods they occur.

The treatment of corporate income taxes also illustrate the case. A tax claim resulting from taxable losses usually does not meet the recognition test. By expensing the related tax effect, the tax rate to the income statement will be affected.

All inclusive concept

Common practice is to include income and expenses fully into the income statement. Holding gains, extraordinary items, even prior year adjustments and other items, which hardly bear any relationship with the current years operations, are recognised in the income statement for the current year. IASC allows for a direct charge or credit to shareholders' equity only in a few specific cases. Effects of retroactive changes caused by changes in accounting policies and effects of changing currency rates on the net assets of foreign entities are the major examples.

In some countries, immediate charge of goodwill to shareholders' equity is acceptable — it even might be common practice — in other countries capitalisation of goodwill and amortisation to income is required (in accordance with the recently issued IASC Statement of Intent). The accounting for goodwill on business combinations is under review in an effort to harmonise different local accounting practices.

Measurement of the elements of financial statements

The IASC Framework mentions four different measurement bases which are employed to different degrees and in various combinations in financial statements: historical cost, current cost, realisable value and present value. The latter two are used, in both the historical cost and the current cost models for accounting, to determine whether carrying amounts of assets will be recovered by future benefits. If such is not the case, provisions have to be made against income.

Open market conditions which might exist on foreign currencies and securities markets might lead to measurement of the related assets at realisable value (= settlement value) even in the absence of sales transaction. In such cases, performance measurement on the basis of positions rather than on effected sales transactions commonly provides more relevant information to users. Trading positions held by financial institutions and by some commodity traders might be treated that way.

Maintenance concept of capital

The IASC Framework distinguishes between financial capital maintenance and physical capital maintenance. Under the first concept, profit is earned if the net assets (valued at cost) increased during the year. The latter recognises profits only if the physical productive capacity (or operating capability) of the enterprise at the end exceeds that capacity at the beginning of the period. The latter concept commonly is used in hyper inflationary economies as profit calculation on the basis of the financial concept is meaningless.

Annex

Framework IASC

Objectives of financial statements	Provision of financial information useful to a wide range of users in making economic decisions
Underlying assumptions	Accrual basis Going concerns
Qualitative characteristics of financial statements	Understandability Relevance (by nature and materiality) Reliability including: - faithful representation - substance over form - neutrality - prudence - realisation True and fair view

Elements	Assets
	   (criteria: control, past events, future benefits)
	Liabilities
	   (criteria: obligations, past events, future resources)
	Equity: residual interest in assets after deducting liabilities
	Income: increases in economic benefit resulting in increases of equity
	Expenses: decreases in economic benefits resulting in decreases of equity

Recognition of elements	Criteria: Probability
	            Measurability
	            including criteria for: set off
	                                       realisation
	                                       matching

Measurement of elements	Historical cost Current cost Realisable value Present value
Concepts of capital maintenance	Financial Physical

Income Statement and Profit Allocation
in the Czech and Slovak Federal Republic

Ladislav Langr

Until recently, accounting in Czechoslovakia (CSFR) had a minor role. Financial statements were intended to show whether or not the economy was keeping pace with the central plan. Enterprises were more interested in ensuring that they followed the directives of the plan than they were in ensuring that their activities were more efficient and effective. The stifling of the market had very severe consequences. The result was prices of raw materials and products which did not correspond to reality. Product prices did not reflect costs and the information contained in financial statements did not provide the information necessary for state planning.

According to CSFR law, accounting is one of the branches of the unified system of social and economic information. Other branches of this system are budgeting of enterprises, calculating, operational review, statistics and financial statements. Financial statements, as part of the state information system, are produced by the enterprise, sent to the statistical bureau network and then used by the central authorities.

More recently, CSFR authorities are encouraging the establishment of new enterprises by creating better accounting conditions for them. This cannot be done without rapid changes in our accounting system. The following rules have, therefore, been adopted for the period of transition to a market economy, i.e. for the years 1990 and 1991:

— The accounting system for private enterprises was devised in July 1990. Private enterprises with less than 25 employees and a taxable profit not exceeding 540 000 Crowns, may use simplified accounting in the form of a cash-book. Double-entry accounting will be obligatory for larger private enterprises, but their financial statements will be simpler than before. They will consist of a simplified profit and loss statement, a balance sheet, and a profit allocation report.

— Other enterprises will use the accounting system which is obligatory for state enterprises, which has recently been adjusted to take account of the needs of joint-stock companies.

The income statement is the most important of the financial statements; it must be presented monthly by all state enterprises, joint-stock companies, co-operatives and joint-ventures. The income statement consists of several sections, but attention is mostly concentrated on "charges and incomes" and "profit and its allocation".

67

The result of the enterprise's operation, i.e. its profit or loss, is measured by comparing charges with incomes for the whole year from 1st January to 31st December.

Charges are itemised in the financial statements according to types, so that production costs in all of the enterprise's activities can be shown. One of the main items is the external cost of materials and services, i.e. the amount paid to purchase the materials or services, including the amounts of materials used, the consumption of fuel and energy, or repairs and maintenance costs. The next main items are, for example, depreciation of fixed assets, staff costs, payroll tax, net interest paid, fines and penalties, transfers to reserves etc. The accruals are itemised according to main groups of items.

Charges and income are accounted for in the period in which the transaction was carried out.

Like charges, incomes are itemised in the financial statements. The first item lists revenues from manufacturing activities i.e. from production, the second from trade activity, and the next from non-productive activity. The other items may include extraordinary revenues. Income is accounted for after the service in question had been carried out or the goods have been finished. Variations in stocks of finished goods and work in progress, and work performed by the undertaking for its own purposes, are also included.

Income must be adjusted for the special tax on turnover. This is similar in principle to VAT, although the rates differ significantly. It is collected by the supplier from the customer, and then paid to the state.

The distribution of profit is determined by a Government Directive. The enterprise must pay tax on its profit, and sometimes also other charges. This tax was 55 per cent of profit, but was increased by Government directive to 65 per cent. However, service industries pay only 20 per cent in tax, joint ventures with at least 30 per cent of foreign capital pay 40 per cent, and other abatements are possible. The payroll tax, which is 50 per cent of staff costs, is charged as a cost and not as an allocation of profit.

Net profit can be allocated to the enterprise's funds: the development fund, reserve fund or social and cultural fund, to name just a few. The costs of entertaining can be paid only from profit after taxation, once the obligatory allocation to other funds has been made. One section of the income statement lists profit, and in some cases also general subventions from the state budget, the allocation of profit into the funds, and other items. Further data on allocations to funds can be found in independent statements on the sources and uses of the funds.

Fund accounting used to be a basic concept in the CSFR economy. For example, the social and cultural fund of state enterprises must be filled by certain minimum obligatory allocations from profit. The allocated amount corresponds to 2 per cent of the gross amount of wages paid in the year in question. This fund is used by enterprises to assist staff to pay for lunches, holidays or flats. The social and cultural fund can be used only by agreement with the trade union.

Instructions given in the plan determine the allocation of the development fund. In addition, there are several other ways of forming the fund. For example, by the transfer of the amount of capital corresponding with the depreciation charge for fixed assets. This sum is exempt from taxation, as it is transferred from the operational sphere to the investment sphere to encourage the improvement of the enterprise. Until recently, this capital was taken from the enterprise and distributed to enterprises and industries according to the plan. Today, the enterprise may not be deprived of the capital which it has produced. The development fund is used to cover the cost of investments, research and development.

The reserve fund is formed by allocations from profit which matches or exceeds the level of fixed minimum fund balance given in the plan. This fund is used to cover the losses and sudden changes in the financial situation of the company, and sometimes also to fill the development fund and other funds.

An enterprise may uses its profit to create even more funds. Retained profit can now be transferred to be used next year rather than turning it over to central authorities as in the past.

Joint ventures in CSFR need only create the reserve fund, and are not obliged to create any other fund. They are subject to the same accounting rules as state enterprises.

These changes should establish the legislative conditions suitable for the transition to a market economy. The joint-stock company law and private enterprise law have already been passed, some amendments to the business code have been made, providing a sound basis for the establishment of joint-stock companies, private enterprises and various types of corporation, for example limited or unlimited companies, limited partnerships and consortia. Some changes have also been introduced into the joint venture law and state enterprise law. The tax law amendments and financial economy directives are being discussed.

The privatisation process is underway. The Government's approach to it, as well as the liberalisation of prices and the forthcoming convertibility of CSFR currency, have given rise to numerous discussions. The establishment of financial markets and the changes in the banking and insurance industries are also significant steps.

All of these changes are sure to influence the role of accounting. First of all, accounting will have to regain the functions essential in a market economy. The current dependence on the state statistical system and central plan can no longer be tolerated. Accountants will need to become accustomed to internationally recognised standards, principles and regulations and, above all, to the requirement that accounts give a true and fair view of an enterprise's financial affairs. Special attention will need to be paid to the essential accounting concepts, going concern, consistency, prudence and accruals. These concepts are already at the heart of CSFR accounting, but now they must be adapted to new conditions. The valuation of assets and liabilities is important and attention to its methods will be necessary.

A new law on auditing is in preparation and an independent body for audit firms and auditors will be established.

Co-operation with international institutions, individuals countries and advisory firms will be invaluable. For example, France has assisted in the preparation of new accounting rules. Great Britain has enabled our experts to come to London to study accounting issues. CSFR has been a member of the UN Intergovernmental Working Group of Experts on International Accounting and Reporting Standards since 1989. These and various other contacts with institutions and experts from abroad help us to become acquainted with accounting in a market economy.

The transfer to a market economy has caused many changes to CSFR accounting and financial statements. The aim is to modify our financial statements and auditing and accounting practices according to EC Directives, so that our accounting methods can be harmonised with the methods used in other European Countries.

Specific Accounting Rules for Joint Ventures

David Cairns

The purpose of this paper is to describe IASC's International Accounting Standard 31 on Financial Reporting of Interests in Joint Ventures.

Recent years have seen a rapid growth in the number of international joint ventures. This has raised two important accounting issues:

— Under what accounting requirements should the joint venture itself report, particularly where there are substantial differences in the accounting and reporting requirements in the countries of each venturer? The answer to this question depends on whether the joint venture is a reporting entity under the accounting requirements of the host country; and

— How should each venturer report its interest in the joint venture in its financial statements?

IASC's project on joint ventures

IASC began its project on joint ventures in 1983. It published draft proposals in 1986 (Exposure Draft E28, Accounting for Investments in Associates and Joint Ventures) which were revised in 1989 in Exposure Draft E35, Financial Reporting of Interest in Joint Ventures. The IASC Steering Committee dealing with this project met in September 1990 to consider the comments on E35 and prepared a revised text which was approved by the Board in November (IAS 31).

IAS 31 recognises that joint ventures take many different forms and structures. It identifies three broad types — jointly controlled operations, jointly controlled assets and jointly controlled entities — which are commonly described as, and meet the definition of, a joint venture.

The existence of a contractual arrangement establishing joint control is fundamental to the existence of a joint venture. It helps to distinguish interests which involve joint control from investments in associates in which the investor has significant influence (see International Accounting Standard 28, Accounting for Investments in Associates). Activities which have no contractual arrangement establishing joint control are not joint ventures for the purposes of this statement.

The contractual arrangement may take the form of a contract between the venturers or minutes of discussions between the venturers. In some cases, the arrangement is incorporated in the articles or other by-laws of the joint venture. Whatever its form, the contractual arrangement is usually in writing and deals with such matters as:

— The activity, duration and reporting obligations of the joint venture;
— The appointment of the board of directors or equivalent governing body of the joint venture and the voting rights of the venturers;
— Capital contributions by the venturers; and
— The sharing by the venturers of the output, income, expenses or results of the joint venture.

The contractual arrangement establishes joint control by identifying those decisions which require the consent of a specified majority of the venturers. Such a requirement ensures that no single venturer is in a position to control unilaterally the activity.

The contractual arrangement may identify one venturer as the operator or manager of the joint venture. The operator does not control the joint venture but acts within the financial and operating policies which have been agreed by the venturers in accordance with the contractual arrangement and delegated to the operator. If the operator has the power to govern the financial and operating policies of the economic activity, it controls the venture and the venture is a subsidiary of the operator and not a joint venture.

Jointly controlled operations

The operation of some joint ventures involves the use of the assets and other resources of the venturers rather than the establishment of a corporation, partnership or other entity, or a financial structure that is separate from the venturers themselves. Each venturer uses its own property, plant and equipment and carries its own inventories. It also incurs its own expenses and liabilities and raises its own finance, which represent its own obligations. The joint venture activities may be carried out by the venturer's employees alongside the venturer's similar activities. The joint venture agreement usually provides a means by which the revenue from the sale of the joint product and any expenses incurred in common are shared between the venturers.

An example of a jointly controlled operation is where two or more venturers combine their operations, resources and other expertise in order to manufacture, market and distribute jointly a particular product, such as an aircraft. Different parts of the manufacturing process are carried out by each of the venturers. Each venturer bears its own costs and takes a share of the revenue such share being determined in accordance with the contractual arrangement.

In respect of its *interests* in jointly controlled operations, each venturer includes in its accounting records and recognises in its separate financial statements and any consolidated financial statements:

— The assets that it controls and the liabilities that it incurs; and

— The expenses that it incurs and its share of the income that it earns from the sale of goods or services by the joint venture, in accordance with International Accounting Standard 18, Revenue Recognition.

Because the assets, liabilities, income and expenses are already recognised in the separate financial statements of the venturer, no adjustments or other consolidation procedures are required in respect of these items when the venturer presents consolidated financial statements.

Separate accounting records may not be required for the joint venture itself and the joint venture may not prepare financial statements. However, the venturers may prepare management accounts so that they may assess the performance of the operation.

Jointly controlled assets

Some joint ventures involve the joint control, and often the joint ownership, by the venturers of an asset which has been contributed to or acquired by the joint venture and which is dedicated to the purposes of the joint venture. The asset is used to obtain benefits for the venturers. Each venturer may take a share of the output from the asset, which it is free to dispose of as it wishes, and each bears an agreed share of the expenses incurred in common with the other venturers.

These joint ventures do not involve the establishment of a corporation, partnership or other entity, or a financial structure that is separate from the venturers themselves. Each venturer has control over its share of future economic benefits through its share in the jointly controlled asset.

Many activities in the oil, gas and mineral extraction industries involve jointly controlled assets; for example, a number of oil production companies may jointly control and operate an oil pipeline. Each venturer uses the pipeline to transport its own product in return for which it bears an agreed proportion of the expenses of operating the pipeline. Another example of a jointly controlled asset is where two enterprises control jointly a property, each taking a share of the rents received and bearing a share of the expenses.

In respect of its interest in a jointly controlled asset, each venturer includes in its accounting records and recognises in its separate financial statements and any consolidated financial statements:

— Its share of the jointly controlled asset, classified according to the nature of the asset rather than as an investment. For example, a share of a jointly controlled oil pipeline is classified as property, plant and equipment;

— Any liabilities which it has incurred, for example those incurred in financing its share of the asset;

— Its share of any liabilities incurred in common with other venturers in relation to the joint venture;

— Any income from the sale or use of its share of the output of the joint venture, together with its share of any expenses incurred by the joint venture; and

— Any expenses which it has incurred in respect of its interest in the joint venture, for example those related to financing the venturer's interest in the asset and selling its share of the output.

Because the assets, liabilities, income and expenses are already recognised in the separate financial statements of the venturer, no adjustments or other consolidation procedures are required in respect of these items when the venturer presents consolidated financial statements.

The treatment of jointly controlled assets reflects the substance and economic reality and, usually, the legal form of the joint venture. Separate accounting records for the joint venture itself may be limited to those expenses incurred in common by the venturers and ultimately borne by the venturers according to their agreed shares. Financial statements may not be prepared for the joint venture, although the venturers may prepare management accounts so that they may assess the performance of the venture.

Jointly controlled entities

A jointly controlled entity is a joint venture establishing a corporation, partnership or other entity in which each venturer has an interest. The entity operates in the same way as other enterprises, except that a contractual arrangement between the venturers establishes joint control over the economic activity of the entity.

A jointly controlled entity controls the assets of the joint venture, incurs liabilities and expenses and earns income. It may enter into contracts in its own name and raise finance for the purposes of the joint venture. Each venturer is entitled to a share of the results of the jointly controlled entity, although some jointly controlled entities also involve a sharing of the output.

A common example of a jointly controlled entity is where two enterprises combine their activities in a particular line of business by transferring the relevant assets and liabilities into a jointly controlled entity. Another example arises where an enterprise commences operations in a foreign country in conjunction with the government or other agency in that country, involving the establishment of a separate entity which is controlled jointly by the enterprise and the government or agency.

Many jointly controlled entities are similar to those joint ventures referred to as jointly controlled operations and jointly controlled assets. For example, the venturers may transfer a jointly controlled asset to a jointly controlled entity, for tax or other reasons. Similarly, the venturers may contribute assets which will be operated jointly into a jointly controlled entity. Some jointly controlled operations also involve the establishment of a jointly controlled entity to deal with particular aspects of the activity, for example, the design, marketing, distribution or after-sales service of the product.

A jointly controlled entity maintains its own accounting records and prepares and presents financial statements in the same way as other business entities in conformity with the appropriate national requirements and international accounting standards.

Each venturer usually contributes cash or other resources to the jointly controlled entity. These contributions are included in the accounting records of the venturer and recognised in its separate financial statements as an investment in the jointly controlled entity.

Reporting interests in jointly controlled entities in the consolidated financial statements of the venturer

When a venturer reports an interest in a jointly controlled entity in its consolidated financial statements, it is essential that the venturer reflect the substance and economic reality of the arrangement, rather than the joint venture's particular structure or form. In a jointly controlled entity, a venturer has control over its share of future economic benefits through its share of the assets and liabilities of the venture. This substance and economic reality is reflected in the consolidated financial statements of the venturer when the venturer reports its interests in the assets, liabilities, income and expenses of the jointly controlled entity by using one of the two reporting formats of proportionate consolidation.

A venturer may include separate line items for its share of the various assets, liabilities, income and expenses of the jointly controlled entity (for example current assets, current liabilities, property, plant and equipment, long-term liabilities, income and expenses). Alternatively, it may combine its share of the assets, liabilities, income and expenses on a line by line basis with the similar items in the consolidated financial statements (for example, the share of the jointly controlled entity's cash balance is combined with the cash balance of the consolidated group).

Some venturers use the equity method, as described in International Accounting Standard 28, Accounting for Investments in Associates, to report their interests in jointly controlled entities. IAS 31 does not recommend the use of the equity method because proportionate consolidation better reflects the substance and the economic reality of the venturer's interest in a jointly controlled entity, that is control over the venturer's share of the future economic benefits. Nevertheless, it permits the use of the equity method as an alternative treatment.

The application of proportionate consolidation means that the consolidated balance sheet of the venturer includes its share of the assets that it controls jointly and its share of the liabilities for which it is jointly responsible. The consolidated income statement of the venturer reflects its share of the income and expenses of the jointly controlled entity. Many of the required procedures are similar to those for the consolidation of investments in subsidiaries, as set out in International Accounting Standard 27, Consolidated Financial Statements and Accounting for Investments in Subsidiaries.

Reporting interests in jointly controlled entities in the separate financial statements of the venturer

In many countries separate financial statements are presented by a venturer in order to meet legal or other requirements. Such separate financial statements are prepared in order to meet a number of different needs with the result that different reporting practices are in use in different countries. As a result, IAS 31 does not indicate a preference for any particular treatment.

Transactions between the venturer and the joint venture

When a venturer contributes or sells assets to a joint venture, a question arises as to whether the venturer may recognise any gain or loss arising upon the contribution or sale and, if so, at what amount. Recognition of any portion of such a gain or loss depends on the substance of the transaction, in particular whether a transaction has taken place. While the assets are retained by the joint venture, and provided the venturer has transferred the significant risks and rewards of ownership, the venturer recognises only that portion of the gain or loss attributable to the interests of the other venturers. The venturer recognises the full amount of any loss when the contribution or sale provides evidence of a decline, other than temporary, in the carrying amount of long-term assets or a reduction in the net realisable value of current assets.

When a venturer purchases assets from a joint venture, the venturer does not recognise its share of the profits of the joint venture from the transaction until it resells the assets to an independent party. A venturer recognises its share of the losses resulting from these transactions in the same way as profits except that losses are recognised immediately when they represent a decline, other than temporary, in the carrying amount of long-term assets or a reduction in the net realisable value of current assets.

Reporting interests in joint ventures in the financial statements of an investor

An investor in a joint venture, unlike a venturer, does not share in the joint control of the activity and so does not control a share of the assets and liabilities of the joint venture. The investor's interest has the same substance as an investment in another entity. The investor reports its interest in, and any transactions with, the joint venture in its separate financial statements and its consolidated financial statements in accordance with International Accounting Standard 25, Accounting for Investments, or, if it has significant influence, in accordance with International Accounting Standard 28, Accounting for Investments in Associates.

Operators of joint ventures

One or more venturers may act as the operator or manager of the joint venture activity. Operators are usually paid a management fee for such duties. The fees are accounted for by the joint venture as an expense and are recognised in the operator's income statement in accordance with International Accounting Standard 18, Revenue Recognition.

Accounting Issues Relating to Restructuring, Privatisation and the Development of Financial Markets

Disclosure of Financial Statements

Guy Gelders

In most OECD member countries, any company whose shares are admitted to or quoted on a stock exchange, or are being offered to members of the public, is required:

— when the shares are publicly issued or admitted to the stock exchange, to publish a prospectus, whose purpose is to provide subscribers or the public with information about the shares concerned

— subsequently, to publish an annual financial report and to publish periodical financial statements.

It may be helpful to emphasise that quoted companies represent only a tiny fraction of all companies, probably hardly more than half of one per cent in EC countries, but that they do represent an appreciably higher proportion, though not a predominant one, in their economic significance.

From this standpoint disclosure is conceived essentially in terms of information and protection for shareholders (existing and potential), the company's "owners", which is the only logical reason for requiring it. When shares are distributed among the public, disclosure of financial statements is the only way of informing the public in its capacity as present or potential shareholder.

Disclosure of financial statements in the sense of full information rapidly disseminated, is considered a necessary condition for the capital market to function properly, by helping to determine appropriate share prices and reduce if not altogether eliminate distortions resulting from, e.g., insider trading. From this standpoint, information and disclosure of financial statements are key features of the public capital market.

In a certain number of countries, mainly in western Europe, and especially in terms of EC directives, disclosure of accounts is part of company law and serves the purpose not only of informing shareholders but also of informing and protecting third parties, particularly creditors, when the liability of the associates is limited and when as a result, creditors have no other guarantee than the company's assets. This is the reason why in the EC, the number of companies disclosing accounts now comes to as many as 2.5 million.

Other countries start from the presumption that creditors, and mainly credit establishments, have sufficient bargaining power to obtain the information they need on which to base a lending decision. This view is not shared by the EC, which considers that protecting third-party creditors necessarily involves disclosure of financial statements and their effective availability to *anyone interested.*

The OECD has produced some Guidelines for multinational companies which recommend that:

"Enterprises should, having due regard to their nature and relative size in the economic context of their operations and to requirements of business confidentiality and to cost, publish in a form suited to improve public understanding a sufficient body of factual information on the structure, activities and policies of the enterprise as a whole, as a supplement, in so far as necessary for this purpose, to information to be disclosed under the national law of the individual countries in which they operate. To this end, they should publish within reasonable time limits, on a regular basis, but at least annually, financial statements and other pertinent information relating to the enterprise as a whole, comprising in particular..."

These Guidelines are admittedly intended in the first place for multinational companies as defined in the Guidelines themselves. It is noteworthy that the definitions make no reference either to the company's status in law or to whether or not the company's shares have been quoted on any stock exchange or are otherwise in the hands of the public. Nor do the Guidelines seek to introduce any different practice by multinational companies as opposed to other, single-country companies; they reflect practices that are recommendable for any large company. From this it follows that disclosure of financial statements is part of internationally recognised good practice.

At an April 1986 OECD round table on the disclosure of financial statements, business and trade union representatives drew attention to the importance of disclosure and the effective availability of corporate financial statements for the various objectives a company may have.

OECD countries do in fact have very wide effective disclosure of financial statements for the leading companies. The main differences are in financial statements for smaller companies.

In preparing this address, I enquired in the various countries of central and eastern Europe, operating until recently as planned economies, to ascertain whether the financial statements of their enterprises were being made public or not. I was unable to obtain any affirmative reply. In a planned economy, that seems to be natural. For to the extent that the means of production are in the hands of the State, where there are no financial markets or stock exchange, where the economy of an enterprise is determined by plan directives and in which enterprises have no control over their costs, output or   sales, and therefore have no responsibilities other than those inherent in implementing the authorities' directives, where no enterprise can go bankrupt, where workers have no real power to dispute management decisions, it is to be expected not only that accounts should be geared towards achieving the plan but that the drawing up of accounts and information should be aimed at the sole politically responsible authority, in its simultaneous capacity as owner, creditor, custodian of the plan and entity responsible for the functioning of the economy. From that standpoint, disclosure would serve no useful purpose.

When a planned economy is in a system with no countervailing power from public opinion to the power of the political or administrative authorities to assess prices, economic values, the performance and efficiency of the enterprise, to correct economic mistakes, even irresponsibility or abuse, there is a considerable risk that mistakes, wrong decisions and inefficiency will proliferate, being covered up by successive tiers of the administrative hierarchy.

This brings us on to the political and organisational pattern for society in general as the back-drop to financial disclosure.

Accountancy rules are not just a technical matter: on the contrary, they have institutional and political significance. He also showed how accountancy law fits into the broader concept of the liberal democracy. This seems to me to be particularly true of financial disclosure.

We can all see the difference between:

— keeping books and producing annual accounts in accordance with standards, which may be more or less rigorous or sophisticated, that are essentially geared towards internal management needs or even to certain aspects of control by the authorities (amount of tax payable, adherence to plan), as opposed to:

— disclosure of financial statements in such a way as to enable anyone interested, especially the media, to get at the facts and thus be in a position, even if they are not present or potential shareholders, to assess the management of the company's affairs, its stewardship of the country's resources entrusted to it.

The primary aim of *disclosure* of financial statements is indeed to provide *information* about the financial soundness of the enterprise, in terms of its assets and their being maintained through positive profitability, for others who may be entering into a contract with that enterprise, for instance to provide it with financial assistance in the form of loans, to contract over a long period to purchase from it or supply it, to enter into an agreement to co-operate, to allow lead times for payment, or to commit themselves to it under the terms of a contract of employment.

At a deeper level we can see that political democracy is grounded on disclosure: publicly disclosed laws, open sessions of legislative chambers, open court and tribunal hearings and rulings, budgets and accounts of public authorities. Control by public opinion based on a system of effective disclosure is ultimately the most effective way of ensuring the proper, efficient functioning of the body politic.

What holds true in political democracy is no less true in economic democracy, to ensure the proper functioning and monitor the management of enterprises which, it must be stressed, produce the vast majority of economic goods and services, deploying a substantial share of society's human and material resources and disposing of considerable economic and hence political power.

Shareholders are definitely competent to pronounce upon management, insofar as it is their capital which is being put to work. They need to be in a position to pronounce in full knowledge of the facts, so no important consideration ought to be concealed from them. Similarly, the capital market requires that transactions should be fair and that markets should not be distorted by insider dealing. This means that all important facts and figures have to be disclosed. In the same way too, unless the task is assigned to some administrative authority representing the general interest, and eastern Europe's experience shows just how many pitfalls can bestrew that particular path, the community in general is entitled to expect an enterprise to be run properly and efficiently, using resources efficiently and not wasting or misappropriating them, with no irresponsibility or shirking of responsibilities, and that the enterprise never sets out on the road to bankruptcy. In a political democracy, that task has devolved upon public opinion, assessing on the basis of accurate information.

I should like to conclude that while disclosure of financial statements does have the purpose, in a market economy, of ensuring the proper functioning of enterprises and capital markets, it also has the purpose of ensuring transparency in enterprises, whose social responsibility was appositely pointed out. Only a genuine political democracy can create the right conditions for that.

Disclosure Rules, Prospectuses and Availability
of Financial Statements

Paul Guy

Information needs

Securities and futures regulators are mainly concerned with companies whose securities are distributed to the public or are publicly traded either on an organised exchange or over-the-counter. In certain jurisdictions, public distribution or trading is implied when a company has a certain number of shareholders.

Generally, regulatory bodies apply information (disclosure) requirements at two different stages:

— When securities are distributed to the public;

— After the distribution or listing (continuing disclosure obligations).

Regulatory bodies must ensure that all pertinent information is available to the markets and to investors, either actual or potential. Market prices must reflect all the available information so that they can be efficient and fair.

The work of IOSCO

Since July 1987, the International Organization of Securities Commissions (IOSCO) has been working on two elements of disclosure. One working party was set up to examine issues facing international offers of equity securities and to determine how to facilitate these offerings. Another group was charged with the task of arriving, with the International Accounting Standards Committee and the International Federation of Accountants, at acceptable accounting and auditing standards that could be used in the case of international offering and multiple listings. The work of the two groups are closely related and steps have been taken to ensure that there is adequate coordination.

The group on International Offers has already produced a major report which was made public last September. It identified the main problems facing international offers and recommended a plan of work to arrive at recommendations that would facilitate these offerings. Generally, the Group determined that the offering document (prospectus) should be a short document incorporating by reference the disclosure previously made by the issuer. This brought up the question of continuing disclosure obligations and what, at a minimum, these obligations should be.

Of course, financial statements are a major and fundamental part of the prospectus or of continuing disclosure obligations. At the moment, one major obstacle in the process of making international offers easier is the question of financial statements which, in many cases, must be reconciled to local standards.

This is the reason that IOSCO is trying to arrive at a consensus on acceptable accounting and auditing standards. Important progress has been made in the comparability project (Exposure Draft 32 of IASC) where twenty-one of the twenty-nine proposals to eliminate accounting options have been accepted by IASC without modification. Three E-32 proposals require substantive changes and will be re-exposed for public comments while the five remaining proposals have been deferred pending further work by IASC. Where accounting options still remain, a "benchmark" or preferred treatment was identified but IASC decided not to require a reconciliation to the benchmarks. Securities regulators could however require, as a condition to accept an international securities offering, a reconciliation of the financial statements of the issuer to the benchmark treatment of International Accounting Standards (if it is found to be acceptable at some future point of development).

Besides dealing with the continuation of the comparability project, the Improvements Committee of IASC (of which the Working Party of IOSCO is a member) is now examining the revision of the twenty-one newly accepted standards to ensure that they are sufficiently detailed and complete and contain adequate disclosure requirements. The revision of one accounting standard of "medium complexity" (dealing with construction contracts) is being attempted as a test. This revised standard along with a statement of principles was discussed at a September 1990 meeting of the Improvements Committee.

Finally, the Improvements Committee has identified six areas where additional standards are needed in order to develop a complete set of international accounting standards. Work on those additional standards is also being carried out.

As for auditing issues the Working Group has met with representatives of IFAC in April 1990 to update the action plan set up to address eighteen of the nineteen deficiencies in present International Auditing Standards which have been identified. The one remaining deficiency relates to initial planning and deals with the consideration of internal control and service organisations: that matter has been put on the IFAC list of possible new standards.

As a parallel exercise, IFAC has prepared a draft "Guideline on Ethics for Professional Accountants" which will be discussed with the Working Group. Concerning the issue of the independence of auditors, the SEC has recently completed an extensive analysis of independence requirements in eight different countries which will serve as a basic instrument "to ascertain whether or not it will be possible to come up with a reasonably consistent set of independence requirements that will be appropriate for IOSCO purposes".

New emerging eastern and central european markets

It is important that a public body (either a regulatory body set up to ensure regulation of markets or a government department if no independent body is set up) have the power to approve, recognise, or set accounting standards acceptable in the case of issuers subject to securities or future regulations. This does not mean that this body should effectively set standards. On the contrary, it should rely on an independent standard setting body, if such a body exists or it could approve or recognise other standards. For example, it could recognise the IASC's international standards as those which should be followed by companies subject to the securities on future regulations. These standards are being significantly improved at the moment by the joint effort of IOSCO and IASC. In the same vein the regulatory body could give recognition or approval to international auditing standards. There again, significant changes are being made to these standards by the combined effort of IOSCO and IFAC. The question of independence of auditors and the criteria to be followed are also being looked at.

In any event, it is important for a regulatory body to have the ability to intervene if standards in place are not sufficient to provide investors and potential investors with a true picture of a company's financial condition.

The recognition or acceptance of international standards should be the solution adopted by all economies in transition. This solution should not prevent Eastern and Central European countries from aligning themselves with the European directives. In fact, the two approaches are complementary. Adopting this solution would facilitate the putting in place of sound accounting standards and the integration of issuers from these countries in the international markets.

Disclosure Rules, Prospectuses and Availability of Financial Statements: The Case of the United States

Richard Reinhard

Background

SEC financial statement requirements for foreign issuers

Most offerings — either must comply with US Generally Accepted Accounting Principles (GAAP) or the foreign issuer must prepare financial statements in compliance with a home country comprehensive body of GAAP, reconcile net income and equity to US GAAP, and provide all disclosures required by US GAAP and Regulation S-X (refer to the instructions in Item 18 of Form 20-F).

Form 20-F registration statement for a listing or Form 20-F annual report and other limited offerings — either must conform with US GAAP, except segment disclosures required by Statement of Financial Accounting Standards No.14, or must use comprehensive home country GAAP, reconcile net income and equity to US GAAP, and provide an information content substantially similar to US GAAP and Regulation S-X (refer to the instructions in Item 17 of Form 20-F).

Essentially, disclosures required by US GAAP, but not required under the foreign GAAP need not be furnished. However, notwithstanding the absence of a financial statement disclosure requirement, certain matters may rise to a level of materiality such that they may warrant discussion in the Management's Discussion and Analysis.

Securities act offerings

— Forms F-1 through F-4 make reference to Items 17 and 18 of Form 20-F, as appropriate, for the financial statement requirements of a registration statement.

— Rule 3-19 of Regulation S-X contains the requirements for the periods to be presented Audited balance sheets for the last two years and audited income statements and statements of cash flow for the last three years are required. If the most recent audited balance sheet is over six months old, an unaudited balance sheet as of a date within six months of the effective date is required, accompanied by unaudited income statements and statements of cash flow for the current interim period and the corresponding comparative period of the preceding fiscal year.

Continuous reporting requirements

— An Annual report on Form 20-F is required within six months of the end of the fiscal year. Audited balance sheets for two years and audited income statements and statements of cash flows for three years are required.
— Form 6-K is required to be filed promptly to provide information required to be made public in the home country, filed with a foreign stock exchange or distributed to securities holders.

Auditing requirements

— Auditors must comply with US independence requirements.
— Auditors must comply with US Generally Accepted Auditing Standards in all substantive respects.

Reporting currency for financial statements

— Rule 3-20 of Regulation S-X provides guidance.
— The reporting currency required is the currency of the country where organised or incorporated, or the currency of the primary economic environment in which operations are conducted, i.e., the currency in which cash is primarily generated and expended.
— Dollar convenience translations are only allowed for the most recent year and subsequent interim period using the exchange rate at the most recent balance sheet date or subsequent, if materially different.
— Issuers in countries experiencing hyperinflation (exceeding 100 per cent over the most recent three year period) are required to present supplementary information to quantify the effects of changing prices upon financial condition or results of operations, if the financial statements have not been recast or supplemented to include information on a constant currency or current cost basis.

Financial statements are also required for material equity investees and unconsolidated subsidiaries in Form 20-F and registration statements, and are also required for significant acquisitions in registration statements.

*Accommodations for foreign private issuers inherent in the rules or as administered
by the Staff*

— Age of financial statements — 6 months versus 135 days for US issuers. Timing
   of form filing requirements is longer or more flexible.
— Less stringent requirements on Form 6-K versus Forms 8-K and 10-Q.
— Terminology and captions need not confirm precisely with Regulation S-X.
— Prefiling conferences are welcomed for individual circumstances.

Special considerations for the transition to market economies and privatisation

Development of accounting and auditing standards

The standards of the International Accounting Standards Committee, particularly the
benchmark standards, could serve as a useful tool in the rapid development of a comprehensive
set of national accounting standards.

Auditing and independence standards developed by the International Federation of
Accountants could be utilised to develop national standards.

Revaluation of enterprises to be privatised

In many cases historical costs may not be relevant or determinable for enterprises
being privatised.

A balance sheet based on revalued amounts may be the most reasonable approach in
such circumstances.

In privatisation, not involving a European company, the SEC staff determined that it
would not object if the reconciliation to US GAAP did not include the effects of the initial
revaluation.

Other companies considering or intending to enter the US securities markets should
consult with the SEC staff concerning their particular circumstances with respect to the
possibility of similar accommodations.

*Relevance of historical income statements for enterprises previously operating in
centrally planned economies*

In certain circumstances historical income statements of enterprises may have limited
relevance to investors, particularly if there have been substantial changes in the operating
environment or if an enterprise's products or services were previously subject to only
limited competition from products or services of other enterprises.

Although the SEC staff has not yet been asked to address the possibility of
accommodations in this regard, the staff encourages potential registrants to discuss
individual circumstances.

Evaluation Rules: Assets and Liabilities

Wienand Schruff

Introduction

This paper examines the problems which can arise from a restatement of balance sheet items and how they could be solved. In the former German Democratic Republic, (GDR), the restatement of balance sheet items is affected by three major changes in the economic system which took place in the so-called first treaty of state and which became effective July 1st, 1990:

— The unification of the economies of the Federal Republic of Germany and the German Democratic Republic by which the GDR has committed itself to introduce the market economy system and the rules thereto as currently enforced in the FRG.

— The introduction of the Deutsche Mark as the single official currency in the GDR.

— The introduction of the West German social security system in the GDR.

This paper deals only with the introduction of a market economy system while accounting issues arising from the translation of the balance sheet drawn up in East Mark into Deutsche Mark are left aside. In practice however, the difficulties arising from the translation into Deutsche Mark are of significant importance.

Characteristics of balance sheet items in centrally planned economies

Long-term asset and inventories usually are carried at historical cost less depreciation where applicable. Valuation rules therefore seem to be similar to those applied by western companies. Historical cost in a centrally planned economy, however, is based on state controlled fixed prices and, therefore, not comparable to prices in market economies.

In the GDR, under the rules of foreign trade monopoly, additional charges have been made for goods imported from Western countries according to the shortage of foreign currency reserves. In addition, long-term assets have been increased in value several times by government decree.

The straight-line method is used to depreciate assets which have a limited useful life. The period, however, for which depreciation is calculated exceeds the useful life as applied in western countries — by up to 300 per cent:

— Plant buildings in the GDR, for example, have been depreciated over 80 years (in the FRG depreciation usually is calculated on a useful life of 40 years or even 25 years for plant buildings).

— Office machinery in the GDR have been depreciated over 15 years (in the FRG: 5 years).

Depreciation methods and useful life, as well as other valuation rules in centrally planned economies, are subject to governmental regulation which leaves no free choice to enterprises. From a western point of view, estimated useful life seems much too long. However, it most likely corresponds to reality in Eastern European countries where the shortage of new equipment and machinery makes it sensible to repair old machines again and again. In addition, expenditure for general repairs has been accounted for as an increase in the value of the respective assets.

The accrual concept of accounting as well as the concept of prudence have not been applied to financial statements in centrally planned economies. Therefore, provisions for contingent losses, that are expected from the fulfillment of contracts signed before the balance sheet date, as well as provisions for uncertain liabilities and bad debt, have not been accounted for.

Consequences of the transition to a market economy system

Establishing a free market system where prices are determined by supply and demand in connection with the liberalisation of foreign trade, will affect the value of an asset in a former centrally planned economy.

In the GDR, the result will be a decline in the value of assets (plant and machinery, for example) compared to their current book value. In order to obtain a solid base for accounting and future financial statements, a revaluation of assets at the date of privatisation is recommended. The Deutsche Mark Opening Balance Sheet Law requires the drawing up of an opening balance sheet as of 1st July 1990.

In market economies, productivity, quality, and condition, determine the value of an asset as compared to its historical cost.

Assets should, therefore, be revalued by using replacement cost which would arise in a free market had the investor rebuilt the enterprise. This applies to plant, machinery, equipment and inventories. Revaluation by current cost, however, should not be regarded as the beginning of inflation accounting in Germany. It is only permitted for the restatement of balance sheet items in the former GDR.

In some cases, however, replacement will not be likely. As a result of the low level of division of labour in the economy, enterprises comprise several departments and functions that are no longer necessary for their operations. For instance, an enterprise in the transportation sector would itself manufacture screws and other replacement parts for its trucks. From now on, enterprises will have to concentrate on their predominant objectives and will need to close their auxiliary functions. The respective assets are to be accounted for at the net realisable value which could only be estimated at zero.

Another important problem arises in the context of accounting for land. Possession of land will be a significant base for evaluation of the credit standing of privatised enterprises. Western creditors usually request mortgages as a security. In countries where land is still the property of the state, it will be necessary to transfer the property rights to the enterprises. In some cases, land may be regarded as the only valuable asset. This leads to the question of how to determine the adequate value of land when there is no functioning real estate market.

The Deutsche Mark Opening Balance Sheet Law requires the use of the fair market value of the respective land for the opening balance sheet. Government guidelines require that the value of land as per square meter is to be calculated by multiplying the average price of land in the Federal Republic of Germany by certain coefficients representing the different conditions such as size of the town, infrastructure, and location, as well as contamination of the respective ground.

The results calculated by applying these guidelines, however, do not represent market values, because a market has not yet crystallised. As far as the purchase of land is concerned, it is common practice to include a specific proviso in the purchase contracts which allows both parties the right to review the price within reasonable time (one year, for example) in light of further development of market values.

On the liabilities side, accruals should be made for uncertain liabilities in order to present a true and fair view of the company's financial position. In the context of restructuring, additional liabilities will be caused by the dismissal of employees which seems to be indispensable but will require compensation payment.

The revaluation of assets and the recognition of liabilities which are uncertain in terms of value and date of payment but are definitely caused before the balance sheet date (July 1st, 1990) can lead to a capital deficit or even to a negative amount of equity. A large number of enterprises will experience this result. Without a specific accounting rule, they would have to go bankrupt. To resolve these problems and to balance the financial position, a claim for compensation may be entered into the balance sheet on the assets side according to the Deutsche Mark Opening Balance Sheet Law. It will be payable by the parent company which, in most cases, is 100 per cent state-owned and controlled by the governmental trustee (Treuhandanstalt). A compensation claim, however, may only be entered into the balance sheet by permission of the parent company, if certain criteria are met.

On the other hand, some enterprises will report a surplus in their opening balance sheet which will be payable to the governmental trustee to compensate liabilities and claims on the national level. Today, it cannot be foreseen whether this system will be balanced or not.

Conclusion

The revaluation of balance sheet items of enterprises in former centrally planned economies will, in a large number of cases, reveal the bad shape and the poor standard of these enterprises. The problems arising from the transition towards a market economy system, however, should not be seen as resolvable by means of accounting policies. In general, a debt restructuring and even a discharge of debt by the former state bank seem to be necessary. The main objective, or task, of the future is the contribution of capital and management know-how.

Valuation Rules: Assets and Liabilities
The Case of Hungary

Maria Borda

Introduction

The objective of this paper is to highlight the differences between present Hungarian accounting valuation procedures and the Generally Accepted Accounting Principles in developed market economies. It describes the important legal developments to accommodate privatisation and highlights the present business valuation practice and its limitations. Specific problems of accounting valuation for financial reporting are also described.

Legal framework for privatisation

The past few years have witnessed major economic changes in Hungary. Commercial banks were established and a series of new laws were enacted. In addition, the reopening of the Stock Exchange and the abolition of the administrative regulation of wages and salaries were undertaken in a drive to establish a market-based economy and to develop a uniform market for commodities, labour and capital. In order to realise the prospective advantages of market development, to encourage entrepreneurial activity and to increase the profit-making ability of the national economy, it is essential to bring the Hungarian national economy into the world market. Besides increasing exports to developed capitalist countries it is of the utmost importance to acquire foreign capital, and along with it modern technology. Joint ventures are generally considered to be one of the most important vehicles of privatisation and foreign investments.

The new legislation

Today, Hungary has the most developed legal framework for privatisation and joint ventures in Eastern Europe. In the past two years, the following laws have come into effect:

1989:   Law No. VI/1988 on Business Associations (Company Law)

Law No. XXIV/1988 on Investments by Foreigners in Hungary

Law No. XIII/1989 on Transformation of State-Owned enterprises and companies

Valuation Decree No. 30/1989

1990   Law No. VI/1990 on Securities and Stock Exchange

Law No. VII/1990 on National Property Agency

The *Law on Business Associations* permits Western-type corporations based on share ownership and limited liability. The *Law on Foreign Investments* guaranties the repatriation of earnings by foreigners in their own currency. It provides special tax benefits in favour of foreigners. This, and the Unified Entrepreneurs' Profit Tax, ensures five-year tax holidays for companies with foreign participation of more than 30 per cent of the capital of a company in manufacturing or in the hotel industry.

The *Transformation Law* encourages the privatisation of viable state-owned enterprises.

The *Valuation Decree* establishes the principles of initial share pricing and net asset valuation.

To create the conditions for a market-driven economy, the Stock Exchange plays a very important role. The National Assembly passed the bill on the circulation of securities and on the stock exchange and *Law No. VI/1990 on Securities and Stock Exchange* came into force on March 1990[1].

Under the provisions of the Transformation Law, a National Property Agency (State Assets Management Agency) was established. The *Law on National Property Agency* came into force on March 1990. This Agency is the policy advisory and review body in Hungary's privatisation process. It has a wide range of functions: monitoring and approving the transformation process and foreign investment; ensuring that state assets are sold for "fair" prices; acting as the executive in the selling process for State-owned enterprises; administering the state's continuing ownership rights. The decisions of this body determine the success, acceptance and effectiveness of the privatisation and the overall restructuring of the Hungarian economy. Its policies should be open and fair and help the managers of transforming state enterprises to act in the interest of the national economy.

In 1990, the first privatisation action programme was approved. It extended to twenty large state-owned companies and eleven thousand restaurants and retail stores of small and middle sizes.

Valuation rules for privatisation

The Law on the Transformation of Business Organizations and Companies provides valuation and other rules for the transformation of state-owned companies into business associations, declaring simultaneously the principle of legal succession. Furthermore, it provides rules for the transformation of a company into another type of company including mergers and split ups.

Common rules of Transformation Law

The common rules concern all transforming organisations, including state enterprises, other state-owned economic bodies, the enterprises of certain legal entities, ancillary companies (subsidiaries), cooperatives, business associations except for certain business unions, self-employed artisans and private tradesmen.

According to these common rules:

— A transformation balance sheet containing the valuation approved by the new owners is drawn up to reflect the realistic market value of operating assets.

— The transformation balance sheet must be audited by an independent chartered accountant, registered by the Ministry of Finance.

— A closing balance sheet as of the date of transformation is drawn up, supported by an inventory, including the distributed profit in accordance with the profit tax law. The accumulated retained earnings must include the amount of net profit. The balance sheet can not contain any transitory items such as prepaid services.

— The difference between the asset value shown on the closing balance sheet versus that on the transforming balance sheet shall be charged to accumulated retained earnings.

— The transforming balance sheet includes the revalued assets and liabilities of the transforming organisation and the amount of owners' equity accepted by the new owners. The owners' equity includes the registered capital, the accumulated retained earnings and the reserve fund. In the course of transformation the value of the reserve may not be increased.

Business valuation practice based on valuation decree

The Valuation Decree 30/1989 was published in order to help the valuation of transforming enterprises.

Selling a state-owned enterprise to a private owner requires a valuation to be made of the net assets involved in the transaction. In contrast to the international business valuation practice, the decree places emphasis on the valuation of individual asset items "likely to be needed in the new company". The purpose of the transformation valuation is to arrive at the "initial" price of the transformed company. It takes account also of such factors as management, organisation, trained labour, intellectual property, innovation, research and supplier infrastructure, customer relationships, market share prospects and goodwill. The new value can be determined as the discounted value of the expected earnings and cash flows, however only as "supplementary information".

Valuation rules for financial reporting

The form and content of financial statements

Bookkeeping and financial reporting requirements are differentiated according to the annual sales revenues of business organisations. If annual sales revenues exceed HUF 250 million, double-entry bookkeeping is required. Below HUF 250 million sales a simplified double-entry bookkeeping, and below HUF 25 million single-entry bookkeeping is allowed. In the last two cases, the financial reporting is also simplified. The following describes the first mentioned financial reporting requirements.

In Hungary, the compulsory closing financial statements for 1989, regulated by order No. 62/1988 (XII.24), include: the Balance Sheet; the Changes of Fixed Assets, the Profit Distribution (for taxation); the Income Statement; in summary as well as in detailed form; the Statement of Costs Detailed by Types; and for the first time as a recommended element the Statement of Sources and Applications of Funds. According to the present practice the three main parts of the Financial Reporting System are the Balance Sheet, the Income Statement, and the Statement of Costs Detailed by Types.

In the present Hungarian accounting practice, the different methods of consolidation such as acquisition or purchase, merger or pooling, or the "former German" method, have not yet been introduced, neither has the equity method for long-term investments. In present practice, participation in other business organisations is valuated at acquisition cost. According to the provision of the new accounting law, if the long-term investment in other companies is less than 50 per cent ownership, the investment should be valuated at acquisition cost. In the case of portfolio investment, the lower of cost or market method is applied. Minority ownership appears on the parent company balance sheet as long-term investment. In compliance with international standards, the new law requires consolidation if the long-term investment represents more than 50 per cent ownership.

Principles and theories behind the accounting valuation

In Hungarian accounting, increases in the market prices of individual assets are not reflected in the valuation of assets on the balance sheet or as gains in measuring net income until the assets are sold. Only sales transactions affect income. The asset valuation in the balance sheet is based on the historical price, whereas liabilities are shown in book value. Consequently, the difference in assets and liabilities equals the realised profit or loss shown in the Income Statement (before tax). The profit is the source of increase in assets between the opening and closing date of the balance-sheet. By using historical cost valuations and the realisation convention, the conventional financial statements fail to reflect the result of management's decisions in the firm's current economic environment.

Current accounting basically meets the requirements of the accruals principle but not in every respect. Effects of business transactions and other events are generally recognized when they occur, independently from cash received or paid. Business transactions are not always recorded in the books and shown in the financial statements of the period to which they relate.

Other basic accounting principles applied by developed market economies, such as going-concern, consistency, substance over form, are also applied. In Western accounting, the concept of prudence exerts a significant influence on the measurement and accounting methods used for the preparation of financial statements. On the one hand it prevents the presentation of non-realised profits and helps to avoid paying tax on uncertain profits. On the other hand, the prudence principle should not be used for the intentional creation of hidden reserves. The Hungarian accounting system does not yet apply the principle of prudence although it appears in the principle of using the lowest possible cost for inventory valuation.

The valuation for financial reporting is based on the principle of historical cost. This does not always meet the requirements of the rapidly changing economic environment and the valuation rules generally accepted in the developed market economies. The last revaluation of fixed assets took place in 1968. The rules applied to the ownership of land differ from those in the West. The inflation rate is substantial. There is no requirement to make provision for doubtful accounts and slow moving inventories.

Particular accounting and valuation problems must be solved when moving from a centralised to a market economy, including:

— There is a need to adopt the lower of cost or market approach to valuation of inventories and marketable securities.

— Depreciation techniques must be expanded beyond the traditional straight line approach.

— It is necessary to develop ways of estimating bad debt expense.

— Greater emphasis should be placed on the marketing function with the expected result of some new and different selling expenses.

— Inflation accounting techniques should be introduced.

— There is a need to establish the accounting methods for long-term investments.

The next Accounting Law, due in 1992, will address these issues.

Valuation rules of assets and liabilities

Property, plant and equipment

Property, plant and equipment are valued at historical cost. For financial reporting no departure from the historical cost basis is permitted. The straightline depreciation methods are used. The norms for depreciation used to be compulsory. Recently they became more flexible, but are still restricted. The new law will bring the depreciation of tangible assets under managerial decision making. Presently, there is no difference between depreciation requirement for financial and tax reporting. This will be introduced by the new law. The interest charges on loans for ongoing investments are capitalised as part of the cost of property and plant. That type of interest charge does not affect the net income of the accounting year. After bringing the plant into operation, the interest charge is recorded as a period expense against the revenues of the period.

In current accounting, the low value, short-lived items are distinguished from fixed assets. Furniture, manufacturing tools and mixtures with acquisition cost lower than 50 000 HUF (US$800) and useful life lower than 3 years, are defined as low value, short-lived items. These are depreciated 50 per cent on first utilisation and 50 per cent in the year of consumption. The new law will eliminate this category of current assets.

Land

Valuation of land depends on how long ago it had been purchased. In the past, it was recorded without value. The unsettled state of land ownership hinders foreign investments in Hungary. The new accounting legislation will solve this problem in accordance with the new real estate law.

Leased assets

In Hungarian practice, the capital lease accounting method is not used. All leases are considered as operating leases. This helps managers in the use of off balance sheet financing. The new law will introduce a requirement for disclosure.

Oil, gas and other mineral resources

In the case of oil, gas and other mineral resources, depletion is based on the value of the natural resource.

Intangible assets

Intangible assets, purchased or self generated, are valued at cost. These may include non-patented know-how reflected in the research and development costs of products, costs of development of computer software, patents, brand names, and good will. Presently, there is no amortisation for intangible assets. This will be legislated by the new law.

Inventories

The valuation of inventories is based on historical costs. The LIFO, FIFO and weighted average method are allowed for the valuation of purchased inventories. There are no special write-downs of inventories for tax purposes.

The self produced inventories are valued at direct cost. The unit cost of finished goods has a major importance in the net income calculation of the period and in the valuation the balance sheet items as well.

In the Hungarian costing system, prime unit cost includes material costs, wage expenditures and, in contrast to the American practice, specific costs of production and selling. These are mostly variable costs. In 1980, the direct unit cost, meaning prime cost as defined above plus factory cost related to machinery, was introduced for the calculation of the cost of industrial products and services. Since 1985, the direct unit cost has also been used in other branches of the national economy with the exception of agriculture. The treatment of work in process under long-term contracts is optional; there is no mandatory method for allocating profits.

Liabilities and provisions

The Hungarian balance sheet does not contain all relevant liabilities relating to a given year's profit — for example profit tax liability or dividend payable. It also does not include all possible accrued liabilities. There is no requirement for the recognition of contingent liabilities and potential losses from pending transactions. Although it is not a legal requirement, professional accountants would make appropriate footnotes. There is no requirement to make provisions for doubtful accounts and for slow-moving or obsolete inventories. According to the new legislation, items which represent a likely loss of value of accounts receivable and slow moving or obsolete inventories, will be reported among the liabilities, such as targeted reserves created from pretax profit.

Taxation. Deferred liabilities

In Hungary, reported income and taxable income are required to be the same. In 1989 the profit tax rate was 40 per cent up to the amount of HUF 3 million and 50 per cent over that limit. In 1990 the tax rate was reduced to 35 per cent up to the amount of HUF 3 million and 40 per cent over that limit. Deferred taxation will be introduced by the new legislation.

Conclusion

In order to facilitate the Hungarian transition from the centrally planned economy to a market driven system and to bring the Hungarian economy into the world market, the problem of accounting reform must be addressed.

Economic developments have made the old accounting model obsolete. There is a need to introduce accounting standards matched with generally accepted accounting principles used in the developed market economies, to comply with international and European Economic Community standards. This will be facilitated by the next accounting law due in 1992.

The legal and economic reforms being undertaken in Hungary will help the development of business valuation techniques, according to the international business valuation standards. They emphasise that the sum of individual asset value items is not equal to the value of the business as a whole. The new accounting law will ensure that valuation rules for financial reporting will be congruent with international requirements, and will ensure appropriate accounting valuations for a market economy.

The Accounting Profession

The Role and Organisation of the Accounting Profession

Brian Smith

This paper highlights the major differences in the role and organisation of the accounting profession between OECD and Central and Eastern European countries focusing on those areas where change is likely to be necessary if the accounting profession is to play a full role in the move to market economies.

Organisation of the accounting profession

The accounting profession in western countries has two main elements, the professionals and accounting firms which provide services in the marketplace and the national professional bodies which support those practitioners and establish the framework within which they operate. In addition, there are multinational professional bodies with an increasing role.

Although the profession is organised differently in each country, there are common characteristics.

The role of the profession

In a market economy, accountants play a key role by acting as independent auditors of financial statements, as tax consultants and as management consultants. Independent auditing plays an important role in the allocation of capital by providing credibility to information used in the capital markets. Users of financial statements need to rely on the information disclosed by enterprises and the independent audit responds to this need.

The services provided in OECD countries, require a high and increasing level of competence and experience. The qualification of auditors is ensured by a combination of legislation and rules established by professional bodies. Other services provided by accountants are generally not regulated and are subject to less restrictive professional rules. Accounting services, including auditing are provided by private sector professionals.

In centrally planned economies, most accountants are employees of industrial enterprises. The senior accountant in an enterprise combines the responsibility for accounting and reporting with that for compliance with regulations and relevant centrally planned objectives. There is no exact equivalent of the accounting profession as understood in OECD countries. Audit procedures are carried out by government authorities or by government related authorised auditing organisations. In the absence of a capital market, the objectives of the audit process are different. The auditing organisations are significantly smaller than in similar sized western economies. There are no significant providers of the other services performed by accounting firms in OECD countries.

The role of the firms

In OECD countries, the relative significance of the individual services varies from country to country and from firm to firm within each country. Many smaller firms focus mainly on accounting and taxation advice. The larger firms perform very little accounting work but provide a wide range of consultancy services in addition to providing audit and taxation advice. The rapid pace of change in Eastern Europe makes theses consultancy services particularly important.

Most of the major international accounting firms have either already established offices in Central and Eastern European countries or have formed joint ventures with local accountants or others as a base for applying for recognition as authorised independent auditors. These international accounting firms make up a significant part of the profession in most countries and have a key role to play in the development of professions in Eastern Europe. In the short term, they will provide experienced manpower for high priority projects assisting in the transition to a market based economy. By providing training for nationals and by giving access to the accumulated experience and methodologies of the firms, a substantial transfer of both standards and technology will occur.

All of the international firms will want to develop national firms which are headed and run by nationals as soon as possible. This will be done through the supervision and training given locally. It will be helped by training and work experience outside the country in the firm's developed offices. This will speed the process of transfer of technology and of specific skills and experience relevant to the country's current needs. As a result it will also speed the process of training nationals to assume leadership roles and replace expatriates as quickly as possible.

The international firms also have an ability to provide services across frontiers and services which are understood and respected by western investors and governments. This is an important characteristic as countries look to obtain significant infusion of funds from western sources.

Organisation of the firms

In all OECD countries, there is a wide variation in size amongst practitioners. Many operate as sole practitioners whilst others operate in small partnerships with a few principals and modest supporting staffs. Services for most medium and larger firms are provided by national firms and national firms closely linked with international firms all of which have more significant resources. The national firms may have a number of offices in the major cities and a structure which provides specialist divisions recognising the more specialised needs of their client base. Generally, the largest firms in any country are the national firms with international links. Again this reflects the nature of the firms client base and the need for both international service and the even wider range of specialist expertise which is available through the sharing of costs and the larger size of the international firms.

Most of the firms are structured as partnerships or as corporations mirroring partnerships in their internal affairs. The partners take direct responsibility for client matters and are supported by an appropriate number of trained staff.

The role of national professional bodies

In OECD and in central and eastern european countries, accountants have formed professional bodies to represent their interests both at national and international level. The great majority of national professional bodies in western countries are self-regulated institutions. They represent their practicing members and operate within a framework which may be established by law but which allows for detailed implementation and administration to be in the private sector. In some countries, some parts of the function of a professional body are assumed or shared by government or by separate bodies.

In addition to representing members in dealings with government, national professional bodies set standards concerning ethics, auditing and accounting, discipline members and set and administer entrance educational requirements, examinations and post qualification eduction. Beyond these basic roles, most institutes establish mechanisms for the exchange of ideas, some perform or commission accounting research and most publish accounting related material.

The majority of professional bodies have an elected committee or council representative of the members which takes policy decisions and provides general oversight. The head of the body is usually elected, although in many cases selected would be a better term.

The council or committee is supported by sub-committees of members covering the various aspects of the body's activities. In addition, there will be a permanent staff of very varying size to implement the decisions taken by the committee and to administer the organisation.

OECD professional bodies differ from those in Central and Eastern Europe both in structure and role. If the accounting profession is to play an effective role in the former centrally planned economies there will need to be significant change.

The role of international professional bodies

Over recent years, multinational professional bodies have been established to develop professional standards at international level and to encourage uniformity between countries.

Most national accounting bodies, including some in Eastern Europe, are members of the International Federation of Accountants (IFAC). Its role is a general representational one for the accounting profession worldwide. It establishes auditing standards and is also producing international standards in other areas such as ethics and education. The Fédération des Experts Comptables Européens (FEE) has a similar role at the European level.

Accounting standards are the role of the IASC, the International Accounting Standards Committee. This body is closely allied to IFAC. Its standards are of particular relevance to those countries which do not have the resources to develop their own standards. Although IASC standards currently permit significant variation in accounting, current exposure drafts start the process of reducing the alternatives.

Assisting in the development of the profession in Central and Eastern Europe

Professional bodies around the world can assist in the development of national professional bodies using their own experience of organisational and administrative matters. An effective professional body is key to an effective profession.

In addition, the professional bodies can give advice on the establishment of standards in all areas, arrange exchanges of personnel, help establish education and training programmes and assist with publications and similar matters. The professional bodies role is that of a facilitator. Most have relatively few resources and will call on the accounting firms to assist.

The most effective way of ensuring the rapid development of a strong accounting profession is to allow free access to the international accounting firms. As indicated above, each of the accounting firms will wish to establish a national firm headed and staffed mainly by nationals as quickly as possible. Expatriates are useful in the development stage and to provide specific and specialised expertise but the strength of the practice is determined by the effectiveness of the national leadership and personnel. These individuals know their country and have a clear interest in its development as well as in the development of the firm of which it is a part.

Summary

The accounting profession is an important element in the economy of all OECD countries. It provides a wide range of services building on its core competence in the adding of credibility to information. It supports the capital markets through its independent audit role.

An effective profession requires a strong national professional body and a wide range of service providers. A mix of national firms with international connections, national firms and smaller practitioners is required to respond to the various needs in the economy. The international firms have a particularly important role to play.

The initiatives to reorganise the accounting profession which have been started in some central and eastern european countries need to be extended and built on. The advice being offered by the international accounting bodies such as IFAC and FEE and by individual professional bodies needs to be expanded. This, together with the input from the accounting firms, should ensure that an effective accounting profession is established as rapidly as possible.

Building the Accounting Profession

Gilbert Gélard

Each country of Central and Eastern Europe has its own history and traditions, admittedly kept out of sight for 45 years in some, but ready to come back to life. Another point is that some of the accountancy developments during those 45 years cannot just be treated as null and void.

The best way of tackling this problem, as Descartes might have suggested, would probably be to divide it up into as many parts as necessary for all of them to be dealt with thoroughly. That is impossible here but the essential questions may nevertheless be raised.

What is a profession?

A profession is a subtle mixture of an expertise and an ethical code. A profession has a social usefulness in a given context. If it enjoys certain prerogatives, those should have the purpose of strengthening its efficiency and its usefulness, and so should never become privileges.

The accountant's expertise

In the context of the central and eastern european countries, the expertise to be inculcated into the future accountant has the special feature that it will need to include a concept of the emerging company, of which the accountant will indeed be one of the co-inventors. In the West, everyone broadly understands what a company is, what a market economy is. Even the nationalised industries, and some of our countries have a great many of those, are always referring implicitly or explicitly to the benchmarks of profit and the market economy for their management, so that the question of who actually owns them becomes a rather secondary one from that standpoint. The accountant merely has to guarantee that the company's measurement or assessment of its profits and assets are valid in terms of a socially recognised reference pattern.

In the central and eastern european countries, the situation will be and already is utterly different. "Company", "corporation" are still untranslatable just now, into attitudes if not into the languages themselves. Yet the yardstick we apply to any economic entity can never be neutral in its effect on how that entity behaves. The accountant will therefore need to be acting somewhat as the company's architect, not solely as an outside observer.

So while patterns will have to be taught that are consistent with the market economy, avowed aim of these countries' new leaders, it would be wrong to be in any way dogmatic about them. There is, after all, no such thing as the perfect market anywhere and what the eastern countries will need to be doing is to acclimatise themselves to a long spell of the provisional.

The accountant's ethical code

Everyone would agree that a professional ought to be independent and all countries have introduced measures, varying quite widely from one to another, to safeguard that independence. Compared with other forms of business practice, all countries subject the professional accountant to numerous restrictions, in recognition of his separate status, on such matters as advertising, holding of capital, how fees are to be invoiced, incompatibility with other functions. It would be tiresome and pointless to go into all of these, but what we would find is that each western country has devised its own pattern, based on law or on self-regulation, that the pattern is by no means set in stone, that each probably has its good points to be learned from and that none is perfect.

How are the central and eastern european countries currently viewing and conceding professional independence? It would probably be fair to say, as Paul Valéry does of liberty, that this is "a word with more value than meaning, a word which sings rather than speaks".

No western accountant frequenting the eastern countries can fail to be struck by what looks to us like the confusion of roles, especially as regards the status of the head of the enterprises's accounting department, who appears to be a sort of alternative managing director, wearing two hats (as inside and outside auditor). A clear-cut distinction between internal and external is certainly going to be one of the prerequisites for the transition to the market economy. The transparency that the market implies clearly requires such a separation between two individuals: the technician, drawing up the accounts with the loyalty of a wage-earner to his managing director, and the auditor, contractual or legal, coming in from outside, completely unbiased, with the expertise and independence to guarantee any third party that the rules of the game have been complied with.

That, though, will be harder to achieve than to propose. There may be a need for transitional arrangements, varying in detail from one country to another, so that the roles are shared out as they should be but accounts can still be prepared and audited during the interim period.

To succeed in building up a profession characterised by a high level of expertise and an ethical code adapted to an evolving society, it will probably be necessary to proceed in stages. My own view is that the most pressing need is to educate, to put candidates through examinations, even if only on the theory, so as to constitute recognised elites who will be able to start practicing. The resulting "informal" profession will then, be in a position to express its views on what pattern of organisation will be most appropriate socially, for itself and for the rest of the economy. Examples if not patterns will be plentiful abroad and each country's emerging profession will be able to pick and choose.

Helping the central and eastern european countries will mean listening carefully to what they have to say. No doubt they have more serious problems than those of their accountancy professions. But accountancy happens to be the area in which we, professionals of the West, can contribute our little brick to the edifice.

The Role and Organisation of the Accounting Profession in Poland

J. Sablik

The accounting profession has important traditions in Poland. The present Polish Association of Accountants (PAA) was founded in 1907. From the beginning, its members were both experts as well as accountants often referred to as "support personnel". This organisational unity ensures the professionalism of our members on all levels of accounting. This is a major difference between PAA and similar organisations in many European countries, but our organisational structure has been shaped by over eighty years of tradition.

Today, in Poland, we have a large organisation with membership of over 130 000. Eighty-five per cent of management and thirty-five per cent of support personnel belong to PAA.

Major changes in this profession took place in 1957, when the Institution of Certified Accountants was established and auditing was made mandatory. The standards adopted at that time were based on western experiences, but had to be adjusted to the command economy with a majority of state owned enterprises.

The 1957 law increased the role and prestige of the profession in Poland. Legal regulations concerning the functions and responsibilities and defining the role and the place in management of Chief Accountant, were instrumental in the development of the profession.

The role and obligations of both Certified Expert Accountants and Chief Accountants determined the areas of activities of the PAA, the most important comprising:

— Training of new employees;
— Mastering skills on all levels of the profession;
— Providing expert advice; and
— Assuring access to professional literature.

Accounting must be in line not only with the management system of the enterprise but also the whole national economy. Polish accounting was, out of necessity, adjusted to the command management. However, through the activities of the Association, and numerous articles in the professional press, accountants were kept informed on progress of accounting in other countries. The changes in the Polish economy do not require starting a profession from scratch. This is the view we often hold in talks with our Western partners. The critical job is to adjust previous experiences to new conditions, mastering the skills, and not starting all over again from zero.

113

The fact that in a two week seminar Polish accountants were trained to perform tasks of World Bank experts, and that the accounting joint venture firms are headed by Polish certified accountants, constitute proof of this.

Polish accountants and the PAA have already significant ties to Europe. PAA membership covers all of the profession but is divided into branches. The National Council of Certified Accountants is a member of IFAC since May 1989, we are members of IFAC. One of the tasks of this group is to popularise world standards of bookkeeping, auditing and EEC directives. In order to adjust our organisation to European standards, we are preparing for the transformation of accountants to the professional level as well as establishing the Chamber of Certified Accountants.

Accounting scientists are active in the Scientific Council of the Association. This group prepared a study "Accounting 2000". We publish theoretical manuscripts, as well as translated international standards. Modern accounting and accounting data processing is the subject of work of PAA Institute, developing software based on western standards.

Accountants employed in enterprises are organised in chapters and groups. They have the opportunity to master their skills in training seminars organised by our district centers. 70 000 accountants participate in such seminars each year. Mastering knowledge on credits, taxes, securities is possible due to the publications of our Center of Training Coordination.

The accountants can expand their knowledge through our "Library" series and "The Accounting Monthly". All accountants and enterprises use our consulting assistance and special expert studies by one of PAA enterprises. Information and commentaries are published in a special series of 17 000 circulation a year, written consultations cover more than 5 000 different issues annually.

The Association cooperates with all world accounting firms which have established Polish operations. PAA is a partner in joint ventures with participation of KPMG-DTG, Moor Stephens — London, and Frielingsdorf & Meklenburg KG — Düsseldorf.

PAA conducts many seminars with KPMG-DTG, Price Waterhouse, Frielingsdorf & Meklenburg.

We are in the final stages of organising a Polish-British Accountants Association.

This summary picture of the organisation of the accounting profession in Poland indicates that the Polish profession is in a strong position to join its European colleagues very soon.

Professional Qualifications of Accountants

John Warne

Background

This paper will first give some facts about Chartered Accountants in the UK, before looking at the implications for countries in Central and Eastern Europe.

In Britain more than one out of every ten graduates entering employment take out an Institute of Chartered Accountants in England and Wales (ICAEW) training contract with a firm of chartered accountants.

Of those graduates who enter training as a chartered accountant, over half have first or upper second class degrees. Of those who enter training, less than 25 per cent have a "relevant" degree, i.e., a degree in, for example, business studies or accountancy as opposed to, say, engineering or classics. Of those who eventually qualify, there is some evidence to show that graduates with a non-relevant degree do better than those with a relevant degree.

Of those who are admitted to the Institute, about 50 per cent leave practice to take up senior finance positions in industry and commerce, i.e., move to management accounting or financial management.

Over half the students with an ICAEW training contract are training with the six largest firms in the UK. It is not uncommon for a larger firm to have ten times more applications each year than it can accept.

From these few statistics, three important conclusions can be drawn:

— In the UK the qualification of Chartered Accountant is seen as a highly attractive starting point for a career in practice or in business.

— What is important is basic ability rather than the subjects studied at University. In other words, the skills needed in a chartered accountant are developed during the three years or so of structured education and training.

— Successful firms see long-term benefit in investing in the provision of training and education for their future members.

This leads to the question: why is the Chartered Accountant qualification seen to be attractive? There seem to be two reasons:

- The potential student is convinced that he will receive a system of education and training that will give him the necessary practical and technical skills to enable him to provide an effective service to his or her employer or firm's client.
- The potential student believes that the theoretical and practical training will be intellectually stimulating and, in the longer term, will provide a good career. And success breeds more success. Graduates want to feel that they belong to a successful profession.

What constitutes a sound system of education and training?

There appear to be four main requirements:
- To qualify as a professional accountant requires much more than preparing for examinations. It involves careful integration of practical training with the acquisition of knowledge. It also involves a conceptual understanding of accountancy and related subjects and the development of analytical and critical skills, so that a student learns to evaluate existing practices of organisations and their future needs.
- The professional accountant must have not only competence, but the highest standards of integrity and independence. These qualities must be developed during training.
- The professional accountant needs a broad understanding of the world in which he operates. He needs a thorough understanding of the role of accounting in business and of the regulatory environment in which business operates. He must be able to communicate with those whom he advises or serves.
- The pace of change is accelerating, and the professional accountant needs to understand that accountancy must respond to changes in public policy and economic circumstances.

What does this mean for the newly liberalised countries of Central and Eastern Europe?

It is important for the western accountancy profession not to assume that the structures we know are the ones best suited to those countries making the transition from a centrally planned to a market economy. Apart from practicing accountants, there will be a need for management accountants employed within enterprises and for a large number of people with a more restricted level of competence, i.e., accounting technicians. The requirement is much more complex than simply producing qualified accountants able to offer independent professional services. Equally, it is important not to overlook the lead-times which will be involved in providing a satisfactory professional infrastructure.

In deciding what system of education and training accountants should have, those concerned with the profession in Central and Eastern Europe need first to decide what they want accountants to perform, i.e., do they want practicing accountants to be able to perform not only attest functions but also give tax and consultancy services? In this they will need to ask how far the role seen for professional accountants will in fact encourage able students to consider a career in accountancy. If accountants are to perform only a narrow regulatory function, then it is unlikely that able students will be attracted into the profession. If accountancy is seen as a qualification which opens many doors, it will attract able students who not only want to spend a career in practice but also those who wish to apply the skills they have acquired to the development of industry and commerce and to economic growth.

As the status of a profession depends on the quality of those who join it, professional bodies in Central and Eastern Europe cannot too soon give thought to the qualifications for admission and to the ways in which they can encourage school leavers to consider a career in accountancy. Concern with the status of the profession also means that education and training is not something that can be delegated to somebody else. The newly formed (or reformed) professional bodies of Central and Eastern Europe will want to take as soon as possible responsibility for the standards of education and training of their future members. This means, perhaps, practical advice and help by the profession in the West about entry requirements and about ways in which these entry requirements can be tested.

Conclusion

i) The accountancy needs of the countries of Central and Eastern Europe are complex, and we need to avoid preconceptions about either structures or professional standards. Western European models are not necessarily the most appropriate. We need to listen to and study carefully the views of colleagues from Central and Eastern Europe before offering suggestions for solutions.

ii) There are longer-term needs as well as short-term problems. In as far as a practicing profession is concerned, its standing will depend on the quality of those it attracts into its ranks.

iii) Quality is more likely to be maintained by a broadly-based profession than one which is closely confined to a regulatory role.

iv) To become a professional accountant a student needs much more than to pass examinations: there must be careful integration of training and education.

v) The professional qualification of an accountant is as much a matter of personal qualities as of practice and theory. Integrity and independence need to be virtues which are accepted and valued by a society. They are also indivisible: professional independence must be independence from government as well as from commercial pressures. This may point to a need for vigorous independent professional associations.

United Nations Activities in Accounting in Eastern Europe and the USSR

Lorraine Ruffing

I. Activities of the Intergovernmental Working Group of Experts on International Standards of Accounting and Reporting

In 1982, the United Nations Intergovernmental Working Group of Experts on International Standards of Accounting and Reporting (ISAR) was created by an ECOSOC resolution. ISAR has three objectives: first, to serve as an international body for the consideration of accounting and reporting issues; second, to make a positive contribution to national and regional standard-setting; third, to take into account the interests of developing countries in the field of information disclosure. In this regard, ISAR is the only group with the potential for balanced geographical representation.

To fulfil the first part of its mandate, the Group has taken upon itself a number of tasks. First, ISAR assesses on a periodic basis the information needs of all users of financial statements including investors, creditors, home and host governments, suppliers, consumers, employees and their representatives and the general public.

Second, ISAR consults international bodies (e.g. EC, OECD, IASC) on the development of international standards and reviews these to ensure that they meet the needs of all users. Where there are gaps, ISAR formulates recommendations. One case in point is accounting of environmental protection measures. These functions require that ISAR engages in basic research rather than merely conducting a "Gallup-poll"-type research on various accounting practices. Too often, standards are formulated in a way to gain acceptance by preparers rather than to meet the needs of users.

Third, ISAR monitors disclosure of information by TNCs and evaluates the extent to which international standards are being applied and the information needs of users are being met. The latest survey (1990) undertaken by UNCTC shows that transnational corporations on average, report only half the information they should. The situation is particularly bad concerning items which are of interest to developing countries such as sales, investments and employment by region or country.

Although the world has changed considerably since the creation of ISAR, in that, TNCs are playing a more positive role in world development and financial reporting has improved, much remains to be done in the areas of harmonisation, adequate disclosure and accounting education. The only region where harmonisation has achieved a modest degree of success is within the European Community. Elsewhere in the world, particularly, in the Pacific Rim, in Africa and in Latin America, differences continue to exist. Added to this are the countries in transition from central planning which must revise their accounting systems and rules in order to serve open market economies.

II. Technical assistance activities in Eastern Europe and the USSR

According to UN procedures, technical assistance activities are usually undertaken at the formal request of a government. During the past two years the Centre has been providing technical assistance to the Czech and Slovak Federal Republic, Poland, Yugoslavia and the USSR in the areas of accounting, joint ventures, foreign direct investment and free enterprise zones. This paper will focus on accounting activities in the USSR.

In June of 1989 the Centre and the USSR Chamber of Commerce organised the Workshop on Accounting for and by East-West Joint Ventures in Centrally Planned Economies. It brought together over 150 people from Government, joint ventures, international accounting firms and academia for the first public discussion of accounting regulations. The Workshop identified problems arising from divergent national accounting regulations; explored ways to improve comparability; and discussed the need for accounting education and training. The Workshop papers have been published in English and Russian under the title *Accounting of and by East-West Joint Ventures* by Lafferty Publications. The Workshop recommended the creation of an international Task Force to assist the Ministry of Finance in the improvement of existing accounting regulations for joint ventures. It also elaborated three curricula for education and training in accounting, with particular emphasis on joint ventures.

The need for accounting reform in the USSR

The pace of East-West business co-operation has been nothing short of phenomenal — at least in terms of the number of registered joint ventures. During the first year (1987) of the new Soviet joint venture law, only 23 ventures were registered, during 1988, an additional 168 could be counted; and by 1 January 1990, others were added, bringing the total to 1 247.

While most joint ventures are still small in terms of the average amount of foreign capital invested, their potential benefits are much larger in terms of their ability to relieve strategic shortages and bottlenecks, to earn or save foreign exchange and to accelerate the transfer of technology and management know-how. So far, however, only 10 per cent of the Soviet joint ventures are fully operational. Start-up operations must overcome many hurdles. Western partners face uncertainties regarding the repatriation of profits, access to raw materials, availability of adequately trained local management personnel and certain incompatibilities in accounting practices.

The last of these factors includes the recognition of revenues, expenses and certain liabilities, depreciation methods, valuation of assets and, most important of all, the determination of profits. The last problem is critical since a profits tax is levied once the joint venture's tax holiday runs out. Of all the problems impeding the successful operation of joint ventures, accounting problems are the ones most easily tackled. International accounting is the language of international business. A common language facilitates interaction particularly among business partners who must be able to understand and evaluate business transactions. Consequently, there is a willingness on the part of Soviet authorities to consider solutions based on internationally accepted accounting standards.

It was this willingness that caused the Soviet authorities to take up the recommendation of the Workshop and create a Task Force of international and Soviet experts to revise the Soviet accounting system in line with the need of an open market economy. This approach differs from that of some countries in Eastern Europe which have sought advice on a bilateral basis or have engaged one of the "Big Six" accounting firms to draft accounting legislation. There are many factors which make a Task Force approach particularly attractive. First, the Government can quickly avail itself of the years of work at a relatively low cost which have been done in various multilateral settings; second, it can avoid favouring one national system or firm over another; third, it can receive advice that is both objective and sensitive to its particular needs.

The Task Force on improvements in accounting for joint ventures

The USSR Ministry of Finance and the UN Center on Transnational Corporations, with the participation of A/O Inaudit convened the first meeting of the international Task Force from 12-14 June 1990 in Moscow. The main objective of the Task Force is to modernise the Soviet chart of accounts used by joint ventures so that it is compatible with international practices.

Scope of work of the Task Force

During the first stage of its work, the revised chart of accounts will be applied to joint ventures; in the second stage it will be extended to the rest of the economy including co-operatives and state enterprises. Such a strategy ensures that accounting reforms take place simultaneously with the economic reforms, if not, ahead of them. The chart of accounts will be modernised using international standards which will bring the differing accounting systems of the USSR and the West closer. However, standards will have to meet Soviet needs as well as those of Western investors; in other words, accounting and reporting must still be consistent with Government objectives.

The task is now to transform that system so that it provides useful information for all the participants in an open market economy. Soviet authorities should not be criticised unduly for not scuttling their system and setting up an accounting standards board to re-write accounting legislation. Such an approach might create havoc among the 3 million accounting technicians, bookkeepers and chief accountants who are responsible for filling in the chart of accounts for their enterprises. Soviet reforms must work within existing constraints.

Even before the creation of the Task Force, the Ministry of Finance considered the problems raised at the June 1989 workshop on accounting. New instructions for accounting for depreciation, capital investments, revenue recognition, financial investments, exchange rate translations, leasing and bad debts were issued on 6 June 1990. Among the main

121

remaining problems yet to be resolved are the matching of revenues with expenses; the calculation of production costs, the calculation of profits and the recognition and valuation of assets and liabilities.

For example, concerning production costs clarification is needed on what is a product cost and what is a period cost; what is a direct cost/indirect costs; fixed cost/variable cost. Basically, Soviet accounting ignores the differences between period costs and product costs. All expenses are accumulated in inventories, which are then overvalued by international standards. This will often result in material differences in profits and losses. A comparative example was developed during the first Task Force meeting illustrating some of the main differences between Soviet and international accounting.

Immediately following the first Task Force meeting, a small drafting group was established to adapt the chart of accounts using international standards as a guide, as well as producing instructions to explain the new methods, a glossary, a preamble containing accounting concepts and supplemental financial statements. The modernisation of the chart will provide trial balances from which financial statements and other accounting reports could be produced to satisfy the needs of various users. Accounting principles and bookkeeping instructions for the following accounts of the Chart of Accounts have been re-written in accordance with the internationally acceptable accounting practices:

— Fixed assets;
— Accumulated depreciation;
— Leaseholds;
— Intangible assets;
— Investment in long-term securities;
— Accounts receivable;
— Notes receivable;
— Advances to suppliers;
— Prepaid expenses;
— Materials and supplies;
— Costs of production;
— Manufacturing overhead;
— Finished goods inventory;
— General and administrative expenses;
— Finance charges;
— Sales;
— Profit and loss;
— Retained earnings;
— Paid-in capital;
— Long-term bank loans;
— Other long-term loans;
— Short-term bank loans.

The new recommended practices would eliminate the existing conceptual differences between Soviet and international practices regarding accounting for assets, liabilities, revenues and expenses. The Task Force will meet in the 2nd quarter of 1991 to complete the new chart. Finally, it will be submitted to the Council of Ministers by the Ministry of Finance.

The Task Force considered another issue which is linked to accounting reform and that is the organisation of the accounting profession in the USSR. Accounting reform will be very difficult to implement without the active support of accountants and bookkeepers throughout the USSR. Soviet accountants must be able to both apply the new rules and to use them to evaluate enterprise performance. This means that the current and future generation of chief accountants and bookkeepers must be trained in the new methods. This can best be done through a well-organised accounting profession.

The first step was already taken in December 1989 when the Association of Accountants was formed. Its members are accountants and other experts some of whom perform audits. At the present time it is trying to establish refresher courses, to advise members, to develop ethical norms and to gather information on the establishment of the profession in other countries.

However, there is still a need to create an accounting organisation which would set educational requirements and professional standards for its members as well as to admit them formally into the profession. One Task Force member outlined the many objectives of an accounting organisation. They include the following:

— To decide on the level of education required before an individual is permitted to become a student of the profession;

— To decide on the nature of theoretical and practical training that should be undertaken in the apprenticeship period;

— To set an examination or licensing process, to determine the level of competency required to become a member of the accounting profession;

— To determine continuing education requirements necessary for continued membership;

— To establish a code of conduct for its members;

— To take measures to insure that the interests of the public are protected;

— To comment on matters of public interest from the standpoint of the accounting profession.

UNCTC and accounting education in the USSR

The Centre has been very active in promoting accounting education in the USSR. As a result of the discussions in its Workshop of June 1989, three curricula were prepared, each oriented to a specific audience.

— Programme One: an intensive academic programme in international accounting for final-year university accounting students;

— Programme Two: accounting workshops for practitioners including joint ventures personnel, accountants, regulators;

— Programme Three: training the trainers or retraining Soviet professors in financial accounting and various aspects of international accounting with emphasis on accounting for joint ventures; this programme would enable Soviet institutions to eventually take over Programmes One and Two.

During 1990, the Centre, six leading Soviet educational institutions and the "Big Six" accounting firms organised Programme One for upper-level university students.

The courses were taught in English and concentrated on financial and financial and management accounting. The international instructors, who were assisted by Soviet accounting professors, found the students well-prepared. New concepts and new terminologies were rapidly assimilated in the two to three week period. In the words of those who evaluated the programme they found that the students "familiarised themselves with international principles and grasped the differences between the Soviet and Western concepts; gained an insight into management accounting which is practically unknown to Soviet accountants; and obtained a good understanding of the nature of auditing".

Programme One will be repeated in 1991 in a number of participating Soviet universities. While Programme One is being taught in English in most cases, there is a need for textbooks which are truly international and which are in Russian.

During 1991 the Centre, with the assistance of the Center for International Accounting Development at the University of Texas and the six participating Soviet universities, will select 120 Soviet accounting professors from all over the USSR to participate in a four month intensive course taught by international accounting professors. These professors will come, in the first instance, from the 20-30 Soviet finance and accounting institutes which train "general" accountants. There are, of course, hundreds of other institutes which train accountants in specific sectors such as trade, oil and gas, mining. The advantage of a broad programme is that the 120 professors will receive the same formation and the same instruction in international accounting. This will enable them to work together more easily in reforming Soviet education because they will be operating from a common understanding. Twenty of the Soviet professors who complete the first phase will then be selected for further study abroad for an additional semester. A number of these persons might stay on for another semester in an accounting firm or in an enterprise in order to gain a working knowledge of accounting practices. These professors would then form a cadre of Soviet trainers who could teach basic courses in financial and management accounting and participate in curriculum reform and development.

It must be recognised that the existing accounting courses in the educational institutions are concerned primarily with the provision of instruction on the operation of the existing accounting system. Therefore, if the system changes, the instruction must change and there must be a vanguard in the universities to do this. But it is not enough that Soviet professors be given the new chart of accounts and the new instructions. They must have an understanding of the concepts behind the new practices. This can hopefully be accomplished with a small group of 120 professors who will then be able to set about the task not only of training future accountants but also of overhauling the curricula in Soviet institutions. This may be a long-term job and not one for the limited resources of the United Nations Center on Transnational Corporations. However, it is expected that other partners will come forward from the international academic community. Therefore, the present UNCTC programme will give the USSR a "quick start" as well as having a sizable multiplier effect. Such a start could help to stabilise the current situation and ensure that the current reforms — both economic and accounting-take root and flourish.

The Standard Setting Process

Accounting Standards Setting:
National, Regional and International Approaches

Rainer Geiger

The success of accounting reforms in central and eastern european countries depends on the development of an appropriate institutional framework for the setting of accounting standards. In the former centrally planned economies, there was no need for such institutions. Ministries in charge of economic planning and controls issued detailed accounting instructions which could be mechanically applied by accountants. The instructions were mainly designed to ensure coherent reporting for planning, statistical and, where relevant, tax purposes. They did not aim at reflecting the economic substance of transactions nor did they seek to give a true and fair view of the situation of the enterprise concerned.

The fundamental reform of accounting systems, which is part of the process of transition to a market economy, not only implies a change of substantive rules but also a change of procedures for elaborating those rules. Lessons can be learnt from experience — successes and failures — with standard setting in the West, at national, regional and international levels. The purpose of this article therefore is to show main features of the institutional framework that has developed within the OECD area, discuss the conditions for effective standards development and highlight the achievements and prospects of international cooperation and harmonisation.

For the purpose of this article the term "accounting standard" is understood in a broad sense: it includes all types of accounting rules and established practices whether of a legal or non-legal nature.

Before discussing institutional features it is appropriate to review the basic rationale for accounting standards.

Why do we need accounting standards?

Raising this question in a circle of accountants who have a vested interest in standards development may appear to be begging the answer. Indeed the existence of standards setting bodies and the proliferation of accounting conferences all over the world seem to suggest an obvious need. We should keep in mind, however, that accounting standards, to the same extent as accounting itself, are not values of their own but serve broader economic and social purposes: they create a basis for confidence in corporate activities and the functioning of financial markets and, provide information for economic decision-making.

Do accounting standards, as presently conceived, fulfil these functions[2]. It is fair to say that the answer is less obvious than it may appear. Present systems show some disturbing features which require critical reflection. Readers of the financial press cannot ignore incidents arising from " creative accounting" where companies have taken advantage of loopholes or uncertainties. Another problem stems from the absence of harmonisation of national standards. The credibility of financial statements suffers when the application of different standards to the same transaction produces widely diverging results. Important elements reflecting the value and the prospects of the enterprise, i.e. its capacity to generate future profits, may not be captured at all in its financial statements, the deficiency of accounting for intangibles being a case in point.

An important constraint of present accounting systems is the time lag involved in producing audited financial statements. Markets and market prospects develop rapidly; when they appear, financial statements may be already out of date and unfit as a basis for sound investment decisions. It has therefore been suggested that in our present economic environment, attention shift from accounting standards for preparers of financial statements to rules allowing the access of corporate raw data through computerised information systems; users could then treat the data according to their own needs[1].

Despite these drawbacks, there is, as yet, no viable alternative to accounting standards for corporate financial reporting. Market forces may play a role in inducing companies to publish comprehensive information about their activities but in the absence of regulatory pressures to conform there would not be sufficient incentives for companies to satisfy the information needs of all categories of users having a stake in the future of the enterprise. Powerful investors and lenders might get the information they need but this is not necessarily true for those who do not have such leverage. Comparable financial information, prepared according to generally applicable standards, remain the best guarantee of fairness in the market place. Corporate accountability to a wide range of users, including the public at large, is a basic feature at least in continental european legal systems. The principles of competition are also ensured by the fair and equal treatment of all categories of investors and other users. Allowing some companies to escape general reporting requirements would give them unfair competitive advantages over those complying with the rules.

Another argument in favour of accounting standards is of special importance to the incipient capital markets in Central and Eastern European countries: the need to build confidence. If the public does not perceive companies to act responsibly if certain categories of investors do not have access to reliable information, capital markets will be undermined in their very infancy. To be trusted information has to be comparable from one company to another, in other words it has to be prepared according to the same set of rules.

If accounting standards form part of the necessary rules of the game for a market economy, what can be done to make them more effective? Whatever the institutional model for standards setting, there are a number of conditions which should be met.

Conditions for effective accounting standards

I should like to make five propositions:

1. *Standards should reflect the needs of all users of financial information.*

This includes all those who need to make informed decisions on the situation , the performance and the future prospects of the enterprise, i.e. investors (actual and potential), employees and their representatives, creditors, suppliers, customers, governments and the public at large. The basic needs of these various groups are identical. All expect information to provide a true and fair view of the enterprise and its activities. This is the reason why published financial statements have to serve as general purpose reports. Certain groups, however, may require special information outside of these reports or benefit from specific forms of communication. This is the case, for example, for shareholders and employees which under certain conditions are given access to information not available to the general public. Special reporting requirements may also be imposed by governments for regulatory purposes such as tax, environment and the application of competition laws; such information will generally be supplied in special purpose reports which may be of a confidential nature.

The companies which prepare financial statements are themselves users of this information for their own purposes in the same way they use the information published by their competitors. Their interests must also be reflected[2]. At the least, excessive requirements (the cost of which outweighs their potential benefits) should be avoided and companies should not be obliged to disclose information harmful to their competitive position.

The best, if not only, way to ensure that users' interests are adequately reflected is to have them participate in the standards setting process. For this purpose users' groups can either be represented on decision-making bodies, participate in consultative groups and/or be given an opportunity to comment in writing on draft standards. The institutional pattern varies among OECD Member countries, but there is a clear trend to expand user participation not only at national but also at regional and international levels. Within the EC, the new Accounting Forum brings together representatives of preparers and users of financial statements and the accounting profession to advise the Commission on technical accounting issues and the need to further develop the framework of European accounting in response to new developments. The International Accounting Standards Committee(IASC) works with a Consultative Group having a similar pattern of representation; this group meets regularly to provide input in the development of international accounting standards.

2. *Accounting standards need to be based on a sound conceptual framework for financial reporting.*

A conceptual framework can fulfil two basic purposes. It can provide guidance for the development of new standards and for the interpretation or revision of existing ones. Even in the absence of standards, the principles it contains will be helpful to preparers and users of financial statements. However,the temptation to turn conceptual frameworks into detailed theoretical accounting models should be resisted. As the US experience shows, excessively detailed projects may be too resource intensive and touch upon questions which, in the end, are a matter of political choice[3].

Conceptual frameworks should be relatively short documents setting out the objectives, concepts and main elements of financial statements. The texts published by the IASC and the United Nations provide useful models in this regard[4].

3. *Financial statements should reflect the economic substance rather than the legal form of thetransactions*

As stipulated in the 4th EC Directive, financial statements should provide a true and fair view of the performance and the financial situation of the enterprise. This principle is of such fundamental importance that it permits, where necessary, deviation from detailed accounting rules provided that the reasons are stated and the effects of the deviation specified. Despite this principle, the legal form of transactions still predominates in many countries. In most cases this does not raise problems as legal forms and economic substance tend to coincide and the legal system itself evolves to reflect the changing nature of commercial transactions. Nevertheless conflicts do occur. For example in long term finance leases substantially all risks and benefits inherent in the property of the leased assets are transferred to the lessee. Under an economic approach the lessee would treat the leased property as an asset in its balance sheet[5]. If, however, legal form is the decisive criteria the asset remains with the lessor as no change in title has taken place. Other examples of potential clashes between legal concepts and economic substance are the definition of parent-subsidiary relationships and certain types of new financial instruments[6].

Accounting can only fulfil its basic objectives to provide information for economic decisions if the substance of the commercial and financial transactions of the enterprise is correctly reflected in the financial statements. The principle of substance over form should apply to both individual financial statements and consolidated accounts.

If financial statements are predominated by tax considerations which deviate from accounting principles, they cannot provide a true and fair view of the performance of the enterprise. The separation between tax and financial reporting is the ideal solution which should be retained at least for consolidated accounts. Where countries believe that for individual financial statements conformity between tax accounts and financial statements should be maintained the EC 4th Directive requires that, wherever financial statements deviate from accounting principles as a result of tax rule, this fact and its effect be disclosed in the notes to the financial statements[7].

4. *Accounting standards need to carry sufficient weight to be effectively implemented.*

Where accounting standards have legal character problems of enforcement normally do not arise. But even where standards are set by non-governmental bodies a minimum of legal backing is necessary to ensure compliance. This can be achieved in various ways. In a number of countries essential disclosure and accounting requirements are enshrined in law. They may be complemented by accounting rules which do not have legal force but are nevertheless widely respected. In other countries (eg. USA and Canada) legislation confers legal backing to standards elaborated by private standards setting bodies. Auditors can play an important role in issuing qualified reports on financial statements which do not comply with generally accepted accounting principles and standards.

The EC Accounting Directives are binding on EC Member states and, after incorporation into the national law of these states, on enterprises established in the EC. International accounting standards lack legal backing. Their application mainly depends on their force of persuasion and the support of the accounting profession. To the extent they reflect common practice, they can serve as points of reference for the acceptance or mutual recognition by national authorities and stock exchanges of financial statements for the purpose of international equity offerings[8].

5. Standard setting procedures need to be flexible so that they can adjust to new developments.

Accounting rules often do not keep pace with a rapidly changing business environment. One obvious case in point is the development of new financial instruments which defies traditional accounting principles and procedures[9]. If financial statements are not to become obsolete as a result of such developments accounting rules and practices have to evolve within relatively short time limits. For this purpose procedures should be flexible moving from general principles to more detailed rules. Trial and error must be permitted to a certain extent and periodic reviews should be built into the system.

Excessively detailed and perfectionist approaches to standard setting may stifle new developments and necessary adjustments. The more detailed the standards are the greater the challenge for inventive accountants and financial engineers to find loopholes in the systems and to evade necessary disclosure.

Flexibility is needed, in particular in a period of economic transition such as that taking place in Central and Eastern European countries. Once the essential disclosure and accounting requirement established, such countries would be well advised to move cautiously on the road of standards setting. The transformation and privatisation of the state-owned sector may require accounting techniques which are different from accounting principles normally applicable to continuing operations. Excessive regulatory burdens on enterprises in particular smaller ones should be avoided. While accounting standards should, in principle, apply to all categories of commercial enterprises it may be necessary to allow, in a period of transition, specific accounting practices, including compliance with home country standards, of enterprises under foreign control. For the immediate future accounting standards will have to be shaped according to local needs. However once the economies of Central and Eastern European countries become more integrated into international market, greater emphasis may shift to international accounting standards. This is another reason why flexibility of standards setting procedures is advisable.

International harmonisation of accounting standards

Created in 1979, the OECD Working Group on Accounting Standards is pursuing efforts to promote harmonisation of accounting practices in order to improve comparability of financial statements throughout the OECD area[10]. The OECD Guidelines for Multinational Enterprises provide a frame of reference for these activities[11]. In the chapter on disclosure of information, the Guidelines set out a list of items to be covered in the published financial statements of multinational enterprises. The aim is to improve " public understanding on the structure, activities and policies of the enterprise as a whole" Multinational enterprises are defined in very broad terms. As stated in paragraph 8 of the introduction to the Guidelines, "they usually comprise companies or other entities whose ownership is private, state or mixed, established in different countries and so linked that one or more of them may be able to exercise a significant influence over the activities of others, and , in particular, to share knowledge and resources with others." The Guidelines are not aimed at introducing differences of treatment between multinational and domestic enterprises. Therefore purely national enterprises with a certain size and complex structure are subject to the same expectations in respect to disclosure of information.

The OECD Guidelines are not legally enforceable. They do not intend to supersede national requirements which remain the yardstick for preparing financial statements. However, where the Guidelines contain disclosure recommendations which go beyond national rules and practice, enterprises are expected to voluntarily supply the information. The Working Group on Accounting Standards conducts periodical surveys of a representative sample of annual reports of multinational enterprises to monitor the degree of compliance with the Guidelines[12].

In summary, the OECD Guidelines:

— are addressed to all categories of companies with complex structure;

— focus on information to be provided in consolidated financial statements;

— set out clear objectives for information disclosure which should meet the needs of all categories of users of financial statements.

The disclosure recommendations they provide are indicative and non exhaustive. They are therefore able to accommodate new developments such as the need for the disclosure of significant risks inherent in new categories of financial instruments[13].

In order to facilitate the use of the Guidelines, OECD has published definitions and explanations of all the accounting terms contained in the chapter on disclosure of information[14]. This includes specific interpretations to reflect special characteristics of the operations of banks and insurance companies[15].

The OECD Guidelines do not contain any standards of evaluation or measurement. It is not the task of the OECD Working Group to elaborate such standards. It can, however, encourage international harmonisation of accounting practices through exchanges of views on national and international developments , comparative studies to explore the advantages and disadvantages of different accounting solutions, roundtables and seminars[16]. The essential function of the Working Group is to provide a forum for discussion bringing together governments and non-governmental groups active in the area of accounting standards[17]. It therefore conducts its activities in close cooperation with international business (represented through the Business and Industry Advisory Committee-BIAC), trade unions (represented through the Trade Union Advisory Committee-TUAC) and the international accounting profession (represented through the IASC and the FEE). In addition, the Working Group on Accounting Standards benefits from the multidisciplinary character of OECD in consulting with other Committees on activities which are relevant to accounting and financial reporting, in particular the Committee on Financial Markets and the Committee on Fiscal Affairs.

The international harmonisation process requires a co-ordinated effort of all concerned. For this reason, close contacts have been established between non-governmental and intergovernmental organisations which are active in this field. The EC Commission plays an important role within the OECD Working Group on Accounting Standards, as well as the United Nations Group of Experts on International Standards of Accounting and Reporting. The three Organisations are represented in the Consultative Group of the IASC. There is a considerable degree of interaction between the four organisations through a complementarity of efforts. The EC directives as well as the IASC Standards, have stimulated the activities of the OECD Group which in turn has provided significant input into the work of the United Nations[18]. The working methods used at OECD have served as a model for the recent creation of the European Accounting Forum, a consultative body to the EC Commission.

Conclusions

Western experience with accounting standards setting may provide valuable lessons to central and eastern european countries seeking to reform their own systems. These countries have the unique chance to build upon positive achievements and to avoid failures and pitfalls. The main driving force of accounting reforms will be the aim to achieve a better market oriented- economic system. For this purpose, a new legal and financial infrastructure is being developed, financial markets will be created and savings mobilised. Better accounting will serves these aims as it builds confidence in the market place.

Western experience also teaches some modesty. Accounting systems are fragile and subject to pressures by various interests, not the least of which are bureaucracies and tax authorities. Institutional mechanisms should be developed to ensure that standard setting procedures are fair and transparent and allow all interested parties to express their views. Essential requirements for accounting and disclosure have to be put rapidly in place to speed up the process of transition. But once this framework is defined, flexibility is needed to accommodate future developments. There are no ready made solutions and countries would be well advise to consider the advantages and disadvantages of different approaches to standards setting before opting for one single solution. While generally applicable accounting standards are the objective, during a period of transition different methods could be allowed to coexist, e.g.specific accounting rules for international joint ventures. Confidence in accounting systems necessarily means confidence in the accounting profession. A competent and independent profession can make a major contribution to the development and application of accounting and auditing standards.

As markets grow and become internationalised a greater convergence of accounting standards is inevitable. Harmonisation still has to overcome many obstacles rooted in national systems and traditions. It requires a continuous and concerted effort at national and international levels. The OECD is pleased to welcome the European countries in transition as new partners in this effort.

Notes and references

1. John Denman, "The Role of a Conceptual Framework," in: *Standard Setting for Financial Reporting,* Princeton, N.J. 1987, p. 57

2. Allan Cook, "The Interests and Needs of Multinational Enterprises," in: *Harmonisation of Accounting Standards - Achievements and Prospects,* OECD, Paris, 1986, p. 20

3. Arthur Wyatt, "The Role of a Conceptual Framework," in: *Standard Setting for Financial Reporting,* prec. p. 44

4. IASC, *Framework for the Preparation and Presentation of Financial Statements,* July 1989; *Objectives and Concepts Underlying Financial Statements,* United Nations, New York, 1989

5. *Accounting for Leases,* Working Document No. 4, OECD, Paris 1988

6. Michael Geary, Image fidèle et prééminence du fond économique sur la forme juridique, in: *Réflexions sur la comptabilité (Hommage à B.d'Illiers),* Paris, 1990, p. 143

7. *The Relationship between Taxation and Financial Reporting,* Accounting Standards Harmonisation Series No. 3, OECD, Paris, 1987

8. See the Article of Paul Guy in the present publication

9. *New Financial Instruments,* OECD, Paris, 1988

10. For a detailed description of the activities of the Working Group on Accounting Standards see Rainer Geiger, "L'harmonisation des normes comptables - Le rôle de l'OCDE", in: *Réflexions sur la comptabilité,* precited, p. 171

11. *International Investment and Multinational Enterprises,* Revised Edition, OECD, Paris, 1984

12. The latest survey was conducted on the basis of the 1989 annual reports: *See Disclosure of Information by Multinational Enterprises: the 1989 Survey,* Working Document No.6, OECD, Paris, 1990

13. Accounting Standards Harmonisation No.6: *New Financial Instruments,* OECD, Paris, 1991

14. *Multinational Enterprises and Disclosure of Information: Clarifications of the OECD Guidelines,* OECD, Paris, 1988; a German version of this text (prepared by M.Nigon) has been published by the Bundesanzeiger Bonn under the title: *Die Publizitätspflicht multinationaler Unternehmen: Erläuterung der OECD Leitsätze,* Köln, 1991

15. Accounting Standards Harmonisation No.4: *Operating Results of Insurance Companies,* OECD, Paris, 1988

16. The last Roundtable Discussions dealt with Accounting for Intangibles Assets (the proceedings are to be published in 1992)

17. A landmark was the organisation, in 1985, of an international Forum on the Harmonisation of accounting standards which brought together, for the first time, at the international level all groups concerned with accouting standard setting- government officials, representatives of national and international standard setting bodies, intergovernmental organisations, representatives of business, trade unions and other users of financial statements and the accounting profession. The proceedings have been published under the title: *Harmonisation of Accounting Standards: Achievements and Perspectives,* OECD, Paris, 1986.

18. *Conclusions on Accounting and Reporting by Transnational Corporations,* United Nations, New York, 1988.

The Reform of Accountancy in Poland

Bozena Lisiecka-Zajac

The main objective of accounting reform in Poland is harmonisation, based on the EEC accounting Directives, with Western accounting principles. Before addressing what this objective consists of and how it can be realised it is important to explain the accountancy system in Poland and its purpose which was the management of the national economy based on central planning.

Following the Second World War, our economy was almost completely ruined. The few surviving enterprises were either so small that they did not keep their books, or used in their book-keeping the accounting system introduced by the German Reich. In 1946 it became possible to prepare and implement the first Polish chart of accounts. This was, in principle, similar to the German model (Schmalenbach). Formally, it was intended only for state commercial and industrial organisations. In practice, it was used by all economic entities including private firms, co-operative etc., irrespective of their type of activity (construction, agriculture, transport etc.). Initially, Polish economic legislation was limited to the establishment of principles for the chart of accounts. The matter of valuation principles, determination of financial result and other standards governing the principles of correct book-keeping was not sufficiently appreciated by the planning authorities. The pre-war Commercial Code of 1934 was the only standard used in this respect.

This Code, was of only limited utility as a standard for state or co-operative organisations, as its provisions were addressed formally to commercial companies (limited liability companies and joint stock companies). For evaluation of correct book-keeping, the Treasury instructions of 1949 on commercial and tax accounts were used, though to a limited extent.

The limited utilisation of these instructions resulted from their objective, i.e., the avoidance of tax evasion by private enterprises. The gap in the legal provisions governing the principles of correct accounting was bridged only in 1954 with the instructions of the Minister of Finance. Hence, the chart of accounts of 1946 and the principles for correct book-keeping of 1954 were the two laws governing accountancy in Poland. These laws were periodically developed and improved.

The accountancy system as developed by the above legislation did not extend to private enterprises, i.e. the non-nationalised sector of the economy. The book-keeping of these units systematically declined. Only seldom did it go beyond recordings of sales and purchases in tax accounts.

Before its current reform, the accounting system applied to the nationalised economy, consisting of a uniform chart of accounts, the branch chart of accounts (applying to specific sectors) and a chart of accounts for the financial statements of economic entities. The present plan is to do away with this system. The Ministry of Finance will issue a uniform chart of accounts which will facilitate the preparation of financial statements by enterprises. The uniform chart of accounts is devised as a basis for preparation of the balance sheet and the income statement according to EEC directives. At the same time regulations for correct bookkeeping will be issued.

The presentation of financial statements is to serve the interests of shareholders, creditors, suppliers, customers, banks etc. and also tax authorities.

The Financial Statements will have to meet the following requirements:

a) information recorded should be divided into reporting periods;

b) all business operations must be covered chronologically and systematically;

c) all information has to be credible i.e. provide a true and fair view of the financial situation and the performance of the enterprise;

d) the legal form and the substance of the transactions have to be reflected;

e) the essence of business operations will be identified irrespective of their form, whilst particular elements of assets, liabilities, revenue and costs, as well as extraordinary profits and losses will be separately disclosed. It is not allowed to compensate assets and liabilities, revenues and costs and extraordinary profits and losses.

f) all material items will be shown separately. Information of lesser significance will be presented in a summary fashion;

g) prudence will be exercised for the evaluation of assets and liabilities and the determination of the financial result;

h) it will be assumed that the activity of the economic subject will be continued (going concern principle).

These principles have been designed in conformity with the fourth EEC directive.

Another element of legislation is the so called "principles for correct bookkeeping". These principles include legislation defining the minimum requirements to be met by:

— books and bookkeeping techniques (manual and computerised),

— book entries, their chronological and systematical order, reporting periods and adequate documentation,

— types of accounts,

— verification and audit of the accounts,

— valuation of assets and liabilities and determination of the financial result (revenues, costs, extraordinary losses and profits), obligation to correct historical value in keeping with the principle of prudence, possible over-estimates (e.g. due to a currency reform and alteration of purchasing power), depreciation of fixed assets and valuation of internally created assets,

— storage and filing of documentation, accounts and financial reports.

The main weakness of Polish accountancy was the result of the basic error of centrally planned economy i.e. the artificially created pricing system. Prices were fixed abitrarily without economic substance. If losses were incurred resulting from arithmetic but not economic comparison of revenue and cost they could be easily compensated by subsidies. To remedy this inadequacy, conditions for the creation of a pricing system compatible with a market economy had to be achieved. This was accompanied by new legislation on demonopolisation and reprivatisation of the economy. As a result prices will become a real measure of value.

As of 1st of January 1991, new principles for correct bookkeeping will come into force. Their main features are as follows:

— Accounting Standards will be set by regulations issued by the Ministry of Finance.

— The accounting principles of the EC Directives will be incorporated.

— Principles for correct bookkeeping will be applicable to all economic subjects, i.e. also to individuals and types of companies participating in free market economy. They will also apply to government departments and local government units, co-operatives, scientific-research institutions etc.

— Some provisions, not covered in EEC directives have been introduced in the text, and other provisions resulting from Polish legislation which is different from that in Western Europe, have been included (to reflect for instance different systems of social security and the creation of welfare and housing funds).

— The principles for correct bookkeeping allow for the over 130 000 accountants currently active to continue their activities without the necessity of re-training. Some of these will become independent accountants due to the greater number of enterprises (establishment of new ones, restructuring of existing ones under reprivatisation and demonopolisation).

Provisions governing bookkeeping and recording techniques have been substantially shortened. Thus the principles of asset valuation and financial measurement, as well as balance sheet preparation and profit calculation, became the substance of the new accounting standards. These standards as well as the required contents of the balance sheet and the income statement are in harmony with the EC directives.

Some new provisions include:

1) The valuation of property components has to reflect their real usefulness at the balance sheet date. The principle of prudence has to be respected.

    This principle applies to the non-monetary components of property (materials, goods, products) as well as to monetary components (cash, securities) expressed in foreign currency, whose price is the exchange rate. It is worthwhile to add that taking into consideration various options (selling rate, buying rate of foreign currency) we have accepted the average rate of exchange determined by the National Bank of Poland.

2) New regulations allow for the creation of reserves in all cases justified by the activity of an economic subject.

Provisions can be created for doubtful debt, and economic risks. They must not be kept in the books for a period fo more than three years.

3) Financial reports are prepared under the supervision of the Central Statistical Office.

4) The list of items of the balance sheet and the income statement set out in the fourth EEC Directive are closely followed. In an annex to the financial statements more detailed information on the activities of the companies will be provided. As in the EEC, this information will contain information on the economic and financial situation of a company, expected developments (results of research and development, effects of investments) status and plans for capital expenditure, size and types of own capital, labour situation etc.

Despite this moving closer to EEC directives there are still problems to solve:

— Although hyper-inflation no longer exists, inflation must be taken into account. Accordingly fixed assets will be periodically revalued.

— Another problem relates to the valuation and methods of classification of fixed assets such as land, arable land, water reservoirs, orchards and plantations, forests and mineral resources.

— As to the consolidation of financial reports there are no solutions for elimination of the intra-group profits and losses. Western solutions seem to be too resource intensive and not sufficiently adapted to the Polish situation.

To conclude, the transformation of Polish accountancy includes another essential change:

The established uniform chart of account and the principles for correct bookkeeping have been supplemented with a number of very detailed rules (instructions of the Minister of Finance) which determine the cost calculation, inventories, cash recording etc. To allow economic entities to select the most suitable solutions, these detailed rules will become voluntary guidelines.

Harmonising Accounting Standards:
The Experience of the European Community

Karel van Hulle

I. Introduction

There is no doubt that the efforts of the European Community to harmonise accounting rules and standards constitute an important element in bringing about an internal market. Cross-border transactions between companies belonging to different Member States is difficult to imagine without the availability of comparable financial data. Reliable financial information is also necessary to further intra-Community trade.

These considerations have become more important since the Community launched its ambitious 1992 project in 1985. However, the Commission did not wait until 1985 to take initiatives in this area. As a matter of fact, harmonisation in the field of accounting and financial reporting started well before the publication of the White Paper on completion of the internal market.

Accounting harmonisation in the Community is part of the company law harmonisation programme. Company law harmonisation is specifically provided for in the EEC-Treaty *(Article 54, sub 3, littera g)* as a means to further freedom of establishment "by coordinating to the necessary extent the safeguards which, for the protection of the interests of members and others, are required by Member States of companies or firms with a view to making such safeguards equivalent throughout the Community."

As part of the company law harmonisation programme, the primary objective of the accounting directives is not the protection of the investors. The accounting directives are there to protect the interests of shareholders, employees and third parties dealing with companies or firms in order to give them equivalent protection throughout the Community. The scope of application of the directives is not limited to companies whose shares are listed on a stock-exchange or to companies which have turned to the capital market, to obtain resources. In principle, the accounting directives apply to all limited liability companies in the Community. As a result, most undertakings involved in intra-Community trade are covered by the harmonisation.

The harmonisation of accounting rules and standards has not been an easy task. People criticising the lack of harmonisation brought about by the Community directives often forget that the level of accounting regulation and practice differed considerably from

Member State to Member State. The harmonisation must be seen in this context. For some Member States, the harmonisation has really been a standard setting. For all Member States, the harmonisation has resulted in the incorporation of accounting standards into legal rules.

The accounting directives

The instrument used in harmonising company law is the directive. A directive is a legal instrument addressed to the Member States. It is binding as to the result to be achieved but leaves to the Member States freedom, as to the form and method for its implementation. When a directive has been transposed into national law it is also binding for companies.

Six directives have so far been adopted in the accounting field.

The *Fourth Council Directive* of 25 July 1978 on annual accounts of limited liability companies (OJ No. L 222 of 14 August 1978) provides the basic structure of accounting in the Community, it deals with the preparation of annual accounts (balance sheet, profit and loss account, notes) which must give a true and fair view of the company's assets, liabilities, financial position and profit or loss. It introduces harmonised lay-outs for the balance sheet and the profit and loss account in order to facilitate comparability. It lays down the valuation rules which are based upon the historical cost principle, allowing Member States to introduce alternative valuation methods, such as a periodic revaluation, a replacement value method or a method of inflation accounting. It also deals with the notes on the accounts, the preparation of the annual report, the publication of the accounting documents and the audit of the accounts. Member States may relieve small and medium-sized companies from certain obligations under the Directive. These derogations relate to the amount of information to be published and to the audit requirement. They do not relate to the valuation rules.

Two amending proposals have been tabled by the Commission and are now before the European Parliament. The first proposal *(OJ No. C 144 of 11 June 1986)* is intended to extend the scope of application to those partnerships and unlimited companies where all the unlimited members are established as limited liability companies. The entities concerned are in fact limited liability companies. An extension of the scope of application to these entities is felt necessary in order to prevent enterprises from escaping the requirements of the accounting directives by changing their legal form.

The second proposal *(OJ No. C 287 of 11 November 1988)* aims at a further harmonisation and simplification of the accounting obligations of small and medium-sized companies. This proposal is part of the Commission's action programme in favour of SME's. Not all Member States have fully used the possibilities in the 4th Directive to exempt small companies from certain requirements. As a result, small companies are subject to a different treatment depending on the Member State in which they are established. Such a situation is likely to cause distortions in competition between companies competing with one another on the basis of unequal financial reporting requirements. This proposal will also allow all companies to prepare and to publish their accounts in ECU.

The *Seventh Council Directive* of 13 June 1983 on consolidated accounts *(OJ No. L 193 of 18 July 1983)* deals with the preparation, publication and audit of consolidated accounts. Consolidated accounts must be prepared where a parent has legal power to control a subsidiary. Member States may also impose consolidation in certain cases of *de facto* control based upon a minority shareholding.

With the adoption of the Fourth and Seventh Directives, the Community disposes of a basic framework in the area of accounting and financial reporting. For certain economic sectors it was felt necessary to adapt these two Directives in order to take account of the specific nature of the activity. The Council therefore adopted on 8 December 1986 a Directive on the annual accounts and consolidated accounts of banks and other financial institutions *(OJ No. L 372 of 31 December 1986)*. Besides introducing a special layout for the balance sheet and the profit and loss account, this Directive contains specific valuation rules for investments, including the possibility for Member States to allow credit institutions to create hidden reserves within certain limits and to show transferable securities which are part of the dealing portfolio in the balance sheet at the higher market value at the balance sheet date (showing the difference between the purchase price and the higher market value in the notes). The Directive must be implemented by Member States before 1 January 1991. A similar directive dealing with the annual accounts and consolidated accounts of insurance companies was proposed by the Commission in 1987 *(OJ No. C 131 of 18 May 1987)*. Following the opinions of the Economic and Social Committee and of the European Parliament, the Commission is now preparing an amended proposal.

The accounts must be audited by a qualified professional who satisfies the criteria of the *Eighth Council Directive* of 10 April 1984 on the approval of persons responsible for carrying out the statutory audits of accounting documents *(OJ No. L 126 of 12 May 1984)*. From 1991 onwards, auditors will be able to practice throughout the Community, as a result of the so-called "mutual recognition" Directive of 21 December 1988 *(OJ No. L 19 of 24 January 1989)*.

Disclosure requirements for branches of companies set up in a Member State by a company established in another Member State or in a third country are the subject of the *Eleventh Directive* of 22 December 1989 *(OJ No. L 395 of 30 December 1989)*. Among the information to be disclosed by a branch are the accounts of the company. as part of the trend towards deregulation, Member States may no longer require the publication by the branch of accounts covering its own activities at least where the branch has been set up by a company from another Member State. A specific directive dealing with the publication of accounting documents by branches of credit institutions and financial institutions was adopted by the Council on 13 February 1989 *(OJ No. L 44 of 16 February 1989)*. It is expected that similar provisions regarding branches of insurance companies will be proposed by the Commission in the near future.

III. The harmonisation process

Harmonisation is not an easy matter. As the harmonisation of accounting standais part of the company law harmonisation programme, the same procedure is followed as in other areas of company law. The procedure starts with the Commission launching a proposal. The proposal is first examined by the Economic and Social Committee and by the European

Parliament. Following the opinion of the European Parliament, the Commission may amend its original proposal. The text will then be discussed in a Council Working Party. Once the Council has reached a common position (for which a qualified majority is necessary), the proposal is then resubmitted to the European Parliament for a second reading before it is finally adopted by the Council of Ministers.

Member States are given several years for the implementation of a directive. If a Member State does not respect the deadline set by a directive for its implementation, the Commission will notify that Member State and remind it of its obligations. If necessary, the Commission will take the Member State concerned before the European Court of Justice. In the same way, the Commission will intervene when a Member State has not correctly implemented the directive or if a Member State does not see to it that the implementing legislation is actually being complied with. As a matter of fact, an important characteristic of the Community harmonisation is that the provisions enacted on the basis of a directive are legally binding.

All parties concerned have a possibility to intervene and to give their comments in the course of the procedure. The accounting profession represented within FEE (Fédération des experts-comptables européens) is closely associated with the preparation of the Commission's proposals and has indeed produced a first draft for most of the accounting directives. The social partners have the possibility to present their views in the Economic and Social Committee and in the European Parliament. This also applies to other users and preparers and to the public at large.

IV. Impact of the harmonisation upon third countries

The EC accounting directive are also of relevance for third countries. It is therefore not surprising that several non-EC countries, particularly in Europe, have followed with great interest the harmonisation within the Community and have indeed incorporated provisions of the accounting directives in their own legislation.

Companies based outside the Community with substantial operations within the Community have no doubt been affected by the EC accounting directives. In addition, several directives have or will attach legal consequences to accounts presented by companies established outside the Community which operate within the Community, provided that these accounts have been prepared in accordance with the Community directives or in a manner equivalent thereto. This is the case under the 7th Directive (Article 11), for the exemption of an intermediate holding company from the obligation to prepare consolidated accounts for its own subgroup. A similar provision applies to banks and other financial institutions in accordance with the Bank Accounts Directive and will also apply to insurance companies. In the same way, the Directive of 13 February 1989 dealing with financial disclosure in relation to branches of credit institutions (Article 3) exempts branches of credit institutions which have their head offices outside the Community from the obligation to publish accounts relating to the activities of the branch if the accounts published by the credit institution have been prepared in conformity with the Bank Accounts Directive or in a manner equivalent thereto. The Eleventh Directive (Article 9) follows a similar approach for branches of limited liability companies from third countries.

The requirement for third country companies to disclose accounts which are at least equivalent to accounts prepared under the Community directives has been introduced in order to avoid discrimination between EC and non-EC companies. Companies established within the Community must indeed disclose accounts prepared in conformity with the accounting Directives.

The Commission is actually examining the notion of equivalence in order to give some guidance to Member States which have to implement the directives and to users and preparers of accounts. The Commission may also want to negotiate with third countries on this issue. As a matter of fact, the concept of equivalence is a concept of European law. It is therefore necessary to develop common criteria.

V. New developments

Following the Conference on the Future of Harmonisation of Accounting Standards within the EC, which the Commission organised on 17/18 January 1990, it was decided to set up a new Accounting Advisory Forum. This Forum will comprise representatives of the various accounting standards setting bodies in Member States as well as representatives of the European organisations of the main users and preparers of accounts, of the accounting profession and of academia. This Forum will advise the Commission about technical solutions for a number of issues which have not been dealt with in the 4th Directive (for instance, foreign currency translation, leasing, long-term contracts, government grants, etc.) or which are undergoing important developments (for instance, intangible assets, new financial instruments). The objective is to make sure that the Community closely follows international developments in the accounting area without losing its own identity. Harmonisation will be furthered by bringing together at regular intervals the main actors which are involved in standards setting at the national level.

The Role of the International Accounting Standards Committee (IASC)

David Cairns

The International Accounting Standards Committee formulates and publishes, in the public interest, accounting standards to be used in the presentation of financial statements. These International Accounting Standards are developed by means of a truly international due process which involves experts in accounting and financial reporting throughout the world.

IASC has the worldwide support and involvement of the accountancy profession, financial analysts, the business community, trade unions, securities regulators and stock exchanges. It works closely with:

— National standard setting bodies;

— Intergovernmental organisations, such as the United Nations Centre on Transnational Corporations, the OECD and the European Commission; and

— Development agencies, such as the World Bank, the International Finance Corporation and various regional organisations.

The business of IASC is conducted by a Board that comprises representatives of the accountancy bodies in thirteen countries and up to four other organisations with an interest in financial reporting. The Board meets regularly an international Consultative Group that includes representatives of users and preparers of financial statements and standard setting bodies as well as observers from intergovernmental organisations.

IASC has approved 31 International Accounting Standards that deal with the substantial majority of topics that affect the financial statements of business enterprises. It is currently working to improve these standards in order to increase the international harmonisation of financial statements and to reduce the costs borne by reporting enterprises that presently have to comply with different accounting requirements in each country in which they operate.

The Relationship between international accounting standards and national accounting requirements

National accounting requirements take many forms. Some countries include detailed accounting requirements in their laws (for example, the Federal Republic of Germany). Some countries have legally enforced requirements laid down by statutory authorities (for example, France and Japan). Other countries have national accounting requirements that are developed by private sector bodies, some of which are under the control of the national accountancy profession (for example, Canada) and others are independent of the profession (for example, the United States). Accounting requirements in some countries are developed and set by a number of different authorities — for example, in the Netherlands the statutory framework of accounting requirements (determined by Parliament based on European Community Directives) is supported by additional guidelines developed by the Council for Annual Reporting (a private sector body).

IASC works closely with those responsible for developing and publishing national (and regional) accounting requirements. Some national standard setting bodies are represented directly on the Board of IASC through their national accountancy bodies. Some are linked through the IASC Consultative Group while contact with others is maintained through liaison with the national accountancy bodies that are members of IASC.

Some countries use international accounting standards directly as national standards (for example, Malaysia, Singapore and Zimbabwe) while others use international accounting standards as the basis for national standards (for example, Egypt, India and Kenya are using all the standards this way whereas some developed countries have used specific international accounting standards to fill gaps in their national requirements). Many countries develop their own requirements in such a way that they conform with International Accounting Standards. For example, the European Community used the IASC standards on consolidated financial statements as the basis for its 7th Directive on consolidated accounts (and IASC used the 7th Directive as the basis for updating its Standard). The French Government used international accounting standards to help it frame statutory requirements for consolidated financial statements. Australia, Canada, the United Kingdom and the United States generally adopt more detailed national standards than international accounting standards whereas other countries, such as Tanzania, have adopted less detailed national standards that generally conform with international accounting standards. More recently, Japan has set up a Commission to explore the possibility of greater conformity between Japanese and international accounting standards. (More information on this topic can be found in IASC's Survey of the Use and Application of International Accounting Standards.)

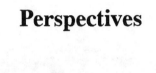

Perspectives

Conclusions and Perspectives

Giorgio Behr

For the countries of Central and Eastern Europe the adaptation of the present economic systems will require new rules to facilitate the transition into market economies. The development of the necessary institutional and legal framework may not keep pace with the changing economic structures and private forces have a major role to play in spurring the transformation process.

In the transition period to a market economy the major difficulty confronting accountants is that the transformation sequence, which includes commercialisation, corporatisation and privatisation of the economy, is vastly accelerated. The countries of Central and Eastern European must initiate this process without having all the necessary elements in place, such as capital markets, investors, etc. It is not a neat process where one phase starts and another is implemented. This is why the adaptation of accounting rules and regulations must quickly serve the changing environment. To delay is to risk wasting valuable time; failure to meet expectations could lead to increased social resistance to change.

The experiences of western market economies related to the development of their accounting systems can be useful for Central and Eastern Europe provided that they are interpreted with caution. There is a need for special regulation to assist the privatisation of enterprises. The example of the privatisation of certain industries, such as telecommunications, in some Western countries may offer valuable lessons.

Accounting reform

Market globalism is bringing about an increasing need for international accounting standards. This however does not obviate the need for the development of standards based on national accounting traditions. Although universally applicable standards on reporting and auditing are an objective for the future, the countries of Eastern Europe need to build accounting systems which respond to their own needs.

The success of the transition process depends in part on a sound conceptual knowledge of the principles of accounting which need to be applied. The essential role of accounting training and research deserves emphasis.

There is a danger that in seeking to assist Central and Eastern European countries in the transition process underway, some individual countries offering advice may be prompted to promote their national standards. A multilateral discussion on possible reforms is probably more constructive than a bilateral one for the reason that the merits of various solutions is more likely to emerge when there is no vested interest in any one national system.

Western intentions to assist in Eastern European accounting development in Central and Eastern Europe must be guided by the needs of the individual countries, which underlines the importance of maintaining contacts of the sort provided for by international colloquia. There must also be on the part of the Central and Eastern European countries, the willingness to seek advice and to have the necessary will and skills to implement the reforms.

The countries' needs and objectives as expressed by them should guide the selection of possible alternatives. That is, familiarity with regional, international, and national regimes should allow a choice suited to their expressed desires. The process of change and the means by which it is achieved is almost as important as the changes themselves. There is a need to listen, to provide opportunity for consultation, and to facilitate the flow of information which is relevant and unbiased. Once the countries concerned have decided on the type of mechanism appropriate to their particular circumstances, the experiences of market economies may provide invaluable assistance.

While giving advice on accounting reform, the overall picture of macroeconomic reform should not be lost sight of. The accounting reforms are directly related to the economic reforms and the new legislation and decrees being passed and implemented must be constant points of reference to ensure that advice on accounting reforms is consistent with the economic reforms being undertaken.

It should be kept in mind that quick fixes which later turn out to be inappropriate may prove difficult to remedy. This has been the experience in some Western economies. New systems should be sufficiently flexible and adaptable to meet changing circumstances. An example is the application of accounting requirements to small and medium sized enterprises. While large enterprises are still predominant, small to medium sized enterprises are likely to be the driving force in the move towards a market economy; these enterprises should not be burdened with excessive regulatory requirements and external financial accounting requirements in their infancy.

Accounting is not an end in itself but has to fulfill a service function. It is part of the process of communicating information to management for the prupose of decision making. But financial accounting is just one dimension in this process and it is important that in introducing new systems recognition be given to current developments in the design and implementation of management information systems, particularly information technology.

The accounting profession

In Central and Eastern Europe, accounting was essentially a bookkeeping function which lowered the level of esteen for the profession. This can be attributed to the centralisation of the economy which did not need accounting as a management tool since decisions were not taken at the enterprise level. The changing role of the profession will require more independence and the state authorised accounting institutions need to be transformed in order to meet the auditing needs of companies. The training and retraining of accountants and managers is essential. There is a need for co-ordination with the legal profession since the legal infrastructure is lagging behind some of the accounting reforms.

Market based economies have an obligation to assist in the development of the accountancy profession in Central and Eastern Europe. However the development of a free standing profession in Central and Eastern Europe is a long term project; the educators have to be educated and the trainers trained. To the extent the countries of the Eastern and Central Europe need accounting expertise immediately they can benefit from the transfer of that know-how. International accounting firms have a role to play in this process and barriers should not be placed in the way in which firms provide services.

It is obvious that there is no single model for the regulation of the profession. One of the topics that clearly requires further reflection relating to the structure of the profession is the potential conflicts of interests that exist with respect to the profession and how the concepts of independence bear on those issues.

In the West a framework of independence has developed which relies on five essential concepts.

- the absence of financial interests, direct or indirect, in the clients which absolutely prohibits the owning of any shares by the auditor in a client organisation;
- a framework of rules prohibiting the existence of family relationships with respect to clients;
- the prohibition against joint business interests between the accounting organisation and their clients;
- the prohibition against auditors assuming decision making responsibility with respect to managerial decisions of the enterprise;
- and lastly, the relationship between fees collected from a single client and the total fees realised by the accounting firm.

Perspectives for co-operation

The discussions highlighted the importance of finding the appropriate balance between reforming, as rapidly as possible, the accounting systems in formally centrally planned economies and the need to move cautiously so as to perserve that which is useful from the former systems and to draw lessons from experiences in the West, particularly some privatisation experiences. Technical assistance, particularly that which leads to a better understanding of international accounting standards, is an important element in preparing these countries to fully adapt to market conditions. Consultations with officials responsible for drafting and implementing the new legislation which will be required can also be provided by the various international and national organisations dealing with accounting. Finally, providing assistance to the countries of Central and Eastern Europe in formulating accounting rules and in training accountants and managers who will be responsible for implenting those rules, can effectively bolster the transformation process.

List of Authors

Giorgio Behr

Conseiller de l'Office Fédéral des Affaires Economiques Extérieures

SWITZERLAND

Vice-Chairman of the OECD Working Group on Accounting Standards

Dr. Maria Borda

International Management Center

HUNGARY

David Cairns

Secretary General
International Accounting Standards Committee

(IASC)

Allan V. C. Cook

Technical Director
Accounting Standards Board for the UK and Ireland

UNITED KINGDOM

Andrew Cunningham

Moore Stephens, Chartered Accountants

UNITED KINGDOM

Maria Dudas

Ministry of Finance

HUNGARY

Rainer Geiger

Deputy Director
Directorate for Financial,
Fiscal and Enterprise Affairs

OECD

Gilbert Gélard

Conseil Supérieur de L'Ordre des Experts-Comptables

FRANCE

Guy Gelders

President
Commission des Normes Comptables

BELGIUM

Chairman of the OECD Working Group on Accounting Standards

Paul Guy	Secretary General International Organisation of Securities Commission (IOSCO)
Prof. Alicja Jaruga	University of Lódz Department of Accountancy POLAND
Ladislav Langr	Ministry of Finance Accounting Methodology CSFR
Herman Marseille	Coopers and Lybrand NETHERLANDS
Dietz Mertin	Treuarbeit AG GERMANY
Richard J. Reinhard	Securities and Exchange Commission UNITED STATES
Dr. Veijo Riistama	Public Accountant FINLAND
Lorraine Ruffing	Intergovernmental Group of Experts on Accounting and Reporting Centre on Transnational Corporations UNITED NATIONS
Jerzy Sablik	Accountants Association POLAND
Ingrid Scheibe-Lange	Trade-Union Advisory Committee to the OECD (TUAC)
Dr. Wienand Schruff	KPMG GERMANY
Brian Smith	Arthur Andersen & Co. UNITED STATES
Karel van Hulle	Commission of the European Communities EEC
John Warne	Institute of Chartered Accountants of England and Wales UNITED KINGDOM
Bozena Lisiecka-Zajac	Ministry of Finance Accounting Department POLAND

WHERE TO OBTAIN OECD PUBLICATIONS – OÙ OBTENIR LES PUBLICATIONS DE L'OCDE

Argentina – Argentine
CARLOS HIRSCH S.R.L.
Galería Güemes, Florida 165, 4° Piso
1333 Buenos Aires Tel. 30.7122, 331.1787 y 331.2391
Telegram: Hirsch-Baires
Telex: 21112 UAPE-AR. Ref. s/2901
Telefax:(1)331-1787

Australia – Australie
D.A. Book (Aust.) Pty. Ltd.
648 Whitehorse Road, P.O.B 163
Mitcham, Victoria 3132 Tel. (03)873.4411
Telefax: (03)873.5679

Austria – Autriche
OECD Publications and Information Centre
Schedestrasse 7
D-W 5300 Bonn 1 (Germany) Tel. (49.228)21.60.45
Telefax: (49.228)26.11.04
Gerold & Co.
Graben 31
Wien I Tel. (0222)533.50.14

Belgium – Belgique
Jean De Lannoy
Avenue du Roi 202
B-1060 Bruxelles Tel. (02)538.51.69/538.08.41
Telex: 63220 Telefax: (02) 538.08.41

Canada
Renouf Publishing Company Ltd.
1294 Algoma Road
Ottawa, ON K1B 3W8 Tel. (613)741.4333
Telex: 053-4783 Telefax: (613)741.5439
Stores:
61 Sparks Street
Ottawa, ON K1P 5R1 Tel. (613)238.8985
211 Yonge Street
Toronto, ON M5B 1M4 Tel. (416)363.3171
Federal Publications
165 University Avenue
Toronto, ON M5H 3B8 Tel. (416)581.1552
Telefax: (416)581.1743
Les Publications Fédérales
1185 rue de l'Université
Montréal, PQ H3B 3A7 Tel.(514)954-1633
Les Éditions La Liberté Inc.
3020 Chemin Sainte-Foy
Sainte-Foy, PQ G1X 3V6 Tel. (418)658.3763
Telefax: (418)658.3763

Denmark – Danemark
Munksgaard Export and Subscription Service
35, Nørre Søgade, P.O. Box 2148
DK-1016 København K Tel. (45 33)12.85.70
Telex: 19431 MUNKS DK Telefax: (45 33)12.93.87

Finland – Finlande
Akateeminen Kirjakauppa
Keskuskatu 1, P.O. Box 128
00100 Helsinki Tel. (358 0)12141
Telex: 125080 Telefax: (358 0)121.4441

France
OECD/OCDE
Mail Orders/Commandes par correspondance:
2, rue André-Pascal
75775 Paris Cédex 16 Tel. (33-1)45.24.82.00
Bookshop/Librairie:
33, rue Octave-Feuillet
75016 Paris Tel. (33-1)45.24.81.67
  (33-1)45.24.81.81
Telex: 620 160 OCDE
Telefax: (33-1)45.24.85.00 (33-1)45.24.81.76
Librairie de l'Université
12a, rue Nazareth
13100 Aix-en-Provence Tel. 42.26.18.08
Telefax : 42.26.63.26

Germany – Allemagne
OECD Publications and Information Centre
Schedestrasse 7
D-W 5300 Bonn 1 Tel. (0228)21.60.45
Telefax: (0228)26.11.04

Greece – Grèce
Librairie Kauffmann
28 rue du Stade
105 64 Athens Tel. 322.21.60
Telex: 218187 LIKA Gr

Hong Kong
Swindon Book Co. Ltd.
13 - 15 Lock Road
Kowloon, Hong Kong Tel. 366.80.31
Telex: 50 441 SWIN HX Telefax: 739.49.75

Iceland – Islande
Mál Mog Menning
Laugavegi 18, Pósthólf 392
121 Reykjavik Tel. 15199/24240

India – Inde
Oxford Book and Stationery Co.
Scindia House
New Delhi 110001 Tel. 331.5896/5308
Telex: 31 61990 AM IN
Telefax: (11)332.5993
17 Park Street
Calcutta 700016 Tel. 240832

Indonesia – Indonésie
Pdii-Lipi
P.O. Box 269/JKSMG/88
Jakarta 12790 Tel. 583467
Telex: 62 875

Ireland – Irlande
TDC Publishers – Library Suppliers
12 North Frederick Street
Dublin 1 Tel. 744835/749677
Telex: 33530 TDCP EI Telefax: 748416

Italy – Italie
Libreria Commissionaria Sansoni
Via Benedetto Fortini, 120/10
Casella Post. 552
50125 Firenze Tel. (055)64.54.15
Telex: 570466 Telefax: (055)64.12.57
Via Bartolini 29
20155 Milano Tel. 36.50.83
La diffusione delle pubblicazioni OCSE viene assicurata
dalle principali librerie ed anche da:
Editrice e Libreria Herder
Piazza Montecitorio 120
00186 Roma Tel. 679.46.28
Telex: NATEL I 621427
Libreria Hoepli
Via Hoepli 5
20121 Milano Tel. 86.54.46
Telex: 31.33.95 Telefax: (02)805.28.86
Libreria Scientifica
Dott. Lucio de Biasio 'Aeiou'
Via Meravigli 16
20123 Milano Tel. 805.68.98
Telex: 800175

Japan – Japon
OECD Publications and Information Centre
Landic Akasaka Building
2-3-4 Akasaka, Minato-ku
Tokyo 107 Tel. (81.3)3586.2016
Telefax: (81.3)3584.7929

Korea – Corée
Kyobo Book Centre Co. Ltd.
P.O. Box 1658, Kwang Hwa Moon
Seoul Tel. (REP)730.78.91
Telefax: 735.0030

Malaysia/Singapore – Malaisie/Singapour
Co-operative Bookshop Ltd.
University of Malaya
P.O. Box 1127, Jalan Pantai Baru
59700 Kuala Lumpur
Malaysia Tel. 756.5000/756.5425
Telefax: 757.3661
Information Publications Pte. Ltd.
Pei-Fu Industrial Building
24 New Industrial Road No. 02-06
Singapore 1953 Tel. 283.1786/283.1798
Telefax: 284.8875

Netherlands – Pays-Bas
SDU Uitgeverij
Christoffel Plantijnstraat 2
Postbus 20014
2500 EA's-Gravenhage Tel. (070 3)78.99.11
Voor bestellingen: Tel. (070 3)78.98.80
Telex: 32486 stdru Telefax: (070 3)47.63.51

New Zealand – Nouvelle-Zélande
GP Publications Ltd.
Customer Services
33 The Esplanade - P.O. Box 38-900
Petone, Wellington
Tel. (04)685-555 Telefax: (04)685-333

Norway – Norvège
Narvesen Info Center - NIC
Bertrand Narvesens vei 2
P.O. Box 6125 Etterstad
0602 Oslo 6 Tel. (02)57.33.00
Telex: 79668 NIC N Telefax: (02)68.19.01

Pakistan
Mirza Book Agency
65 Shahrah Quaid-E-Azam
Lahore 3 Tel. 66839
Telex: 44886 UBL PK. Attn: MIRZA BK

Portugal
Livraria Portugal
Rua do Carmo 70-74, Apart. 2681
1117 Lisboa Codex Tel.: 347.49.82/3/4/5
Telefax: (01) 347.02.64

Singapore/Malaysia – Singapour/Malaisie
See Malaysia/Singapore" – Voir «Malaisie/Singapour»

Spain – Espagne
Mundi-Prensa Libros S.A.
Castelló 37, Apartado 1223
Madrid 28001 Tel. (91) 431.33.99
Telex: 49370 MPLI Telefax: 575.39.98
Libreria Internacional AEDOS
Consejo de Ciento 391
08009 - Barcelona Tel. (93) 301-86-15
  Telefax: (93) 317-01-41
Llibreria de la Generalitat
Palau Moja, Rambla dels Estudis, 118
08002 - Barcelona Telefax: (93) 412.18.54
Tel. (93) 318.80.12 (Subscripcions)
(93) 302.67.23 (Publicacions)

Sri Lanka
Centre for Policy Research
c/o Mercantile Credit Ltd.
55, Janadhipathi Mawatha
Colombo 1 Tel. 438471-9, 440346
Telex: 21138 VAVALEX CE Telefax: 94.1.448900

Sweden – Suède
Fritzes Fackboksföretaget
Box 16356, Regeringsgatan 12
103 27 Stockholm Tel. (08)23.89.00
Telex: 12387 Telefax: (08)20.50.21
Subscription Agency/Abonnements:
Wennergren-Williams AB
Nordenflychtsvägen 74, Box 30004
104 25 Stockholm Tel. (08)13.67.00
Telex: 19937 Telefax: (08)618.62.32

Switzerland – Suisse
OECD Publications and Information Centre
Schedestrasse 7
D-W 5300 Bonn 1 (Germany) Tel. (49.228)21.60.45
Telefax: (49.228)26.11.04
Librairie Payot
6 rue Grenus
1211 Genève 11 Tel. (022)731.89.50
Telex: 28356
Subscription Agency – Service des Abonnements
Naville S.A.
7, rue Lévrier
1201 Genève
Telefax: (022) 738.48.03 Tél.: (022) 732.24.00
Maditec S.A.
Chemin des Palettes 4
1020 Renens/Lausanne Tel. (021)635.08.65
Telefax: (021)635.07.80
United Nations Bookshop/Librairie des Nations-Unies
Palais des Nations
1211 Genève 10 Tel. (022)734.14.73
Telex: 412962 Telefax: (022)740.09.31

Taiwan – Formose
Good Faith Worldwide Int'l. Co. Ltd.
9th Floor, No. 118, Sec. 2
Chung Hsiao E. Road
Taipei Tel. 391.7396/391.7397
Telefax: (02) 394.9176

Thailand – Thaïlande
Suksit Siam Co. Ltd.
1715 Rama IV Road, Samyan
Bangkok 5 Tel. 251.1630

Turkey – Turquie
Kültur Yayinlari Is-Türk Ltd. Sti.
Atatürk Bulvari No. 191/Kat. 21
Kavaklidere/Ankara Tel. 25.07.60
Dolmabahce Cad. No. 29
Besiktas/Istanbul Tel. 160.71.88
Telex: 43482B

United Kingdom – Royaume-Uni
HMSO
Gen. enquiries Tel. (071) 873 0011
Postal orders only:
P.O. Box 276, London SW8 5DT
Personal Callers HMSO Bookshop
49 High Holborn, London WC1V 6HB
Telex: 297138 Telefax: 071 873 2000
Branches at: Belfast, Birmingham, Bristol, Edinburgh,
Manchester

United States – États-Unis
OECD Publications and Information Centre
2001 L Street N.W., Suite 700
Washington, D.C. 20036-4910 Tel. (202)785.6323
Telefax: (202)785.0350

Venezuela
Libreria del Este
Avda F. Miranda 52, Aptdo. 60337, Edificio Galipán
Caracas 106 Tel. 951.1705/951.2307/951.1297
Telegram: Libreste Caracas

Yugoslavia – Yougoslavie
Jugoslovenska Knjiga
Knez Mihajlova 2, P.O. Box 36
Beograd Tel.: (011)621.992
Telex: 12466 jk bgd Telefax: (011)625.970

Orders and inquiries from countries where Distributors
have not yet been appointed should be sent to: OECD
Publications Service, 2 rue André-Pascal, 75775 Paris
Cedex 16, France.
Les commandes provenant de pays où l'OCDE n'a pas
encore désigné de distributeur devraient être adressées à :
OCDE, Service des Publications, 2, rue André-Pascal,
75775 Paris Cédex 16, France.

75880-7/91

OECD PUBLICATIONS, 2 rue André-Pascal, 75775 PARIS CEDEX 16
PRINTED IN FRANCE
(14 91 09 1) ISBN 92-64-13609-6 - No. 45881 1991